]

ISBN-13: 978-1507762424
ISBN-10: 1507762429

BOOKS FROM THE GET 800 COLLECTION FOR COLLEGE BOUND STUDENTS

28 SAT Math Lessons to Improve Your Score in One Month
    Beginner Course
    Intermediate Course
    Advanced Course

320 SAT Math Problems Arranged by Topic and Difficulty Level

320 SAT Math Subject Test Problems Arranged by Topic and Difficulty Level
    Level 1 Test
    Level 2 Test

SAT Prep Book of Advanced Math Problems

The 32 Most Effective SAT Math Strategies

SAT Prep Official Study Guide Math Companion

SAT Vocabulary Book

320 ACT Math Problems Arranged by Topic and Difficulty Level

320 AP Calculus AB Problems Arranged by Topic and Difficulty Level

320 AP Calculus BC Problems Arranged by Topic and Difficulty Level

555 Math IQ Questions for Middle School Students

555 Geometry Problems for High School Students

CONNECT WITH DR. STEVE WARNER

www.facebook.com/SATPrepGet800

www.youtube.com/TheSATMathPrep

www.twitter.com/SATPrepGet800

www.linkedin.com/in/DrSteveWarner

www.pinterest.com/SATPrepGet800

plus.google.com/+SteveWarnerPhD

320 AP CALCULUS BC Problems arranged
by Topic and Difficulty Level

320 Level 1, 2, 3, 4, and 5 AP
Calculus Problems

Dr. Steve Warner

Table of Contents

ACTIONS TO COMPLETE BEFORE YOU READ THIS BOOK

1. Register for my forum

When you get stuck on any AP Calculus problems you can post your questions in the AP Calculus section of my forum. Sign up for free here:

www.satprepget800.com/forum

2. Sign up for AB solutions

Visit the following webpage and enter your email address to receive solutions to all AP Calculus AB problems in this book:

www.thesatmathprep.com/320APCalSup.html

*T*here are many ways that a student can prepare for the AP Calculus BC exam. But not all preparation is created equal. I always teach my students the methods that will give them the maximum result with the minimum amount of effort.

The book you are now reading is self-contained. Each problem was carefully created to ensure that you are making the most effective use of your time while preparing for the AP Calculus exam. By grouping the problems given here by level and topic I have ensured that you can focus on the types of problems that will be most effective to improving your score.

1. Using this book effectively

- Begin studying at least three months before the AP Calculus exam
- Practice AP Calculus problems twenty to thirty minutes each day
- Choose a consistent study time and location

You will retain much more of what you study if you study in short bursts rather than if you try to tackle everything at once. So try to choose about a thirty minute block of time that you will dedicate to AP Calculus each day. Make it a habit. The results are well worth this small time commitment.

- Every time you get a question wrong, **mark it off, no matter what your mistake**.
- Begin each study session by first redoing problems from previous study sessions that you have marked off.
- If you get a problem wrong again, **keep it marked off**.

2. Overview of the AP Calculus exam

There are four types of questions that you will encounter on the AP Calculus exam:

- Multiple choice questions where calculators are not allowed (Section 1, Part A, 28 Questions, 55 Minutes).
- Multiple choice questions where calculators are allowed (Section 1, Part B, 17 Questions, 50 Minutes).
- Free response questions where calculators are allowed (Section 2, Part A, 2 Questions, 30 Minutes).
- Free response questions where calculators are not allowed (Section 2, Part B, 4 Questions, 60 Minutes).

This book will prepare you for all of these question types. In this book, questions that require a calculator are marked with an asterisk (*).

If a question is not marked with an asterisk, then it could show up on a part where a calculator is or is not allowed. I therefore recommend always trying to solve each of these questions both with and without a calculator. It is especially important that you can solve these without a calculator.

The AP Calculus exam is graded on a scale of 1 through 5, with a score of 3 or above interpreted as "qualified." To get a 3 on the exam you will need to get about 50% of the questions correct.

Approximately 60% of the questions on the BC exam are actually AB questions. You will be given an AB subscore based on your performance of these questions. So it is possible to get a high AB subscore while getting a low overall score. In this case you will most likely get college credit for the AB exam, but not for the BC exam.

3. Structure of this book

This book has been organized in such a way to produce maximum results with the least amount of effort. Every question that is in this book is similar to a question that has appeared on an actual AP Calculus exam. Furthermore, just about every question type that you can expect to encounter is covered in this book.

The first part of this book consists of 160 AP Calculus AB questions organized by Level and Topic. An answer key for these problems is included at the end of the section, and full solutions are available as a free digital download at **www.thesatmathprep.com/320APCalSup.html**

The second part of the book consists of 80 AP Calculus BC questions organized by Level and Topic together with full solutions.

At first you want to practice each of the five general math topics given on the AP Calculus exam and improve in each independently. The five topics are **Precalculus**, **Differentiation**, **Integration**, **Limits and Continuity**, and **Series**. Note that you may want to go through the levels from parts 1 and 2 simultaneously. In other words, after completing the Level 1 problems from part 1, you may want to complete the level 1 problems from part 2 before going on to the level 2 problems from part 1.

You will want to progress through the 5 Levels of difficulty at your own pace. Stay at each Level as long as you need to. Keep redoing each problem you get wrong over and over again until you can get each one right on your own.

I strongly recommend that for each topic you *do not* move on to the next level until you are getting most of the questions from the previous level correct. This will reduce your frustration and keep you from burning out.

The third part of this book contains 80 supplemental BC problems with an answer key at the very end. Full solutions to these supplemental problems are not given in this book. Most of these additional problems are similar to problems from the second section, but the derivatives, integrals, and series tend to be a bit more challenging.

Any student that can successfully answer all 160 questions from the first part and all 80 questions from *either* the second or third part of this book should be able to get a 5 on the BC exam.

4. Practice in small amounts over a long period of time
Ideally you want to practice doing AP Calculus problems twenty to thirty minutes each day beginning at least three months before the exam. You will retain much more of what you study if you study in short bursts than if you try to tackle everything at once.

So try to choose about a thirty minute block of time that you will dedicate to AP Calculus every night. Make it a habit. The results are well worth this small time commitment.

5. Redo the problems you get wrong over and over and over until you get them right
If you get a problem wrong, and never attempt the problem again, then it is extremely unlikely that you will get a similar problem correct if it appears on the AP exam.

Most students will read an explanation of the solution, or have someone explain it to them, and then never look at the problem again. This is *not* how you optimize your score on a standardized test. To be sure that you will get a similar problem correct on the actual exam, you must get the problem correct before the exam—and without actually remembering the problem.

This means that after getting a problem incorrect, you should go over and understand why you got it wrong, wait at least a few days, then attempt the same problem again. If you get it right you can cross it off your list of problems to review. If you get it wrong, keep revisiting it every few days until you get it right. Your score *does not* improve by getting problems correct. **Your score improves when you learn from your mistakes.**

6. Check your answers properly

When you are taking the exam and you go back to check your earlier answers for careless errors *do not* simply look over your work to try to catch a mistake. This is usually a waste of time. Always redo the problem without looking at any of your previous work. If possible, use a different method than you used the first time.

7. Take a guess whenever you cannot solve a problem

There is no guessing penalty on the AP Calculus BC exam. Whenever you do not know how to solve a problem take a guess. Ideally you should eliminate as many answer choices as possible before taking your guess, but if you have no idea whatsoever do not waste time overthinking. Simply put down an answer and move on. You should certainly mark it off and come back to it later if you have time.

Try not to leave free response questions completely blank. Begin writing anything you can related to the problem. The act of writing can often spark some insight into how to solve the problem, and even if it does not, you may still get some partial credit.

8. Pace yourself

Do not waste your time on a question that is too hard or will take too long. After you've been working on a question for about a minute you need to make a decision. If you understand the question and think that you can get the answer in a reasonable amount of time, continue to work on the problem. If you still do not know how to do the problem or you are using a technique that is going to take a very long time, mark it off and come back to it later.

If you do not know the correct answer to a multiple choice question, eliminate as many answer choices as you can and take a guess. But you still want to leave open the possibility of coming back to it later. Remember that every multiple choice question is worth the same amount. Do not sacrifice problems that you may be able to do by getting hung up on a problem that is too hard for you.

AB Problems by Level and Topic

Full solutions to these problems are available for free download here:

www.thesatmathprep.com/320APCalSup.html

LEVEL 1: PRECALCULUS

1. Let $f(x) = 3$ and $g(x) = x^4 - 2x^3 + x^2 - 5x + 1$. Then $(f \circ g)(x) =$

    (A) 3
    (B) 22
    (C) 10,648
    (D) $3x^4 - 6x^3 + 3x^2 - 15x + 3$
    (E) $3x^4 + 3x^2 + 3$

2. What is the domain of $k(x) = \sqrt[3]{8 - 12x^2 + 6x - x^3}$?

    (A) All real numbers
    (B) $x < -2$
    (C) $-2 < x < 2$
    (D) $x > 2$
    (E) $x > 0$

3. If $K(x) = \log_5 x$ for $x > 0$, then $K^{-1}(x) =$

    (A) $\log_x 5$
    (B) $\dfrac{x}{5}$
    (C) $\dfrac{5}{x}$
    (D) x^5
    (E) 5^x

12

4. If $g(x) = e^{x+1}$, which of the following lines is an asymptote to the graph of $g(x)$?

    (A) $x = 0$
    (B) $y = 0$
    (C) $x = -1$
    (D) $y = -1$
    (E) $y = -x$

5. Which of the following equations has a graph that is symmetric with respect to the y-axis?

    (A) $y = (x + 1)^3 - x$
    (B) $y = (x + 1)^2 - 1$
    (C) $y = -4x^3 + 2x$
    (D) $y = 2x^6 - 3x^2 + 5$
    (E) $y = \frac{x-1}{2x}$

6. If $f(x) = x^3 + Ax^2 + Bx + C$, and if $f(0) = -2$, $f(-1) = 7$, and $f(1) = 4$, then $AB + \frac{3}{4} =$

    (A) 36
    (B) 18
    (C) -18
    (D) -36
    (E) It cannot be determined from the information given

7. If the solutions of $g(x) = 0$ are -3, $\frac{1}{2}$ and 5, then the solutions of $g(3x) = 0$ are

    (A) -1, $\frac{1}{6}$ and $\frac{5}{3}$

    (B) -9, $\frac{3}{2}$ and 15

    (C) -6, $-\frac{5}{2}$ and   2

    (D)   0, $\frac{7}{2}$ and   8

    (E) -3, $\frac{1}{2}$ and   5

8. If $k(x) = \frac{x^2-1}{x+2}$ and $h(x) = \ln x^2$, then $k(h(e)) =$

    (A) 0.12
    (B) 0.50
    (C) 0.51
    (D) 0.75
    (E) 1.25

LEVEL 1: DIFFERENTIATION

9. If $f(x) = x^2 + x - \cos x$, then $f'(x) =$

    (A) $2x + 1 - \sin x$
    (B) $2x + 1 + \sin x$
    (C) $2x - \sin x$
    (D) $2x + \sin x$
    (E) $\frac{1}{3}x^3 + \frac{1}{2}x^2 - \sin x$

10. If $g(x) = \frac{x+2}{x-2}$, then $g'(-2) =$

    (A) $-\frac{1}{4}$

    (B) -1

    (C) $\quad 0$

    (D) $\quad 1$

    (E) $\quad \frac{1}{4}$

11. If $h(x) = \frac{1}{12}x^3 - 2\ln x + \sqrt{x}$, then $h'(x) =$

    (A) $\frac{1}{3}x^2 - \frac{2}{x} + \frac{1}{2\sqrt{x}}$

    (B) $\frac{1}{4}x^2 - \frac{2}{\ln x} + \frac{2}{3}x^{\frac{3}{2}}$

    (C) $\frac{1}{4}x^2 - \frac{2}{x} + \frac{\sqrt{x}}{2}$

    (D) $\frac{1}{4}x^2 - \frac{2}{\ln x} + \frac{1}{2\sqrt{x}}$

    (E) $\frac{1}{4}x^2 - \frac{2}{x} + \frac{1}{2\sqrt{x}}$

12. The slope of the tangent line to the graph of $y = e^{3x}$ at $x = \ln 2$ is

    (A) $8 \ln 2$
    (B) 8
    (C) $24 \ln 2$
    (D) 24
    (E) 48

13. The instantaneous rate of change at $x = 3$ of the function $f(x) = x\sqrt{x+1}$ is

    (A) $\frac{1}{4}$

    (B) $\frac{3}{4}$

    (C) $\frac{5}{4}$

    (D) $\frac{11}{4}$

    (E) 6

14. $\frac{d}{dx}\left[e^5 + \frac{1}{\sqrt[3]{x^2}} + 11^x\right] =$

15. If $y = x^{\cos x}$, then $y' =$

16. Differentiate $f(x) = \frac{e^{\cot 3x}}{\sqrt{x}}$ and express your answer as a simple fraction.

LEVEL 1: INTEGRATION

17. $\int (x^4 - 6x^2 + 3)\, dx =$

    (A) $5x^5 - 18x^3 + 3x + C$

    (B) $4x^3 - 12x + 3x + C$

    (C) $\frac{x^5}{4} - 3x^2 + 3x + C$

    (D) $\frac{x^5}{5} - 3x^3 + 3x + C$

    (E) $\frac{x^5}{5} - 2x^3 + 3x + C$

18. $\int_{-1}^{2}(3x^2 - 2x)\, dx =$

    (A) 2

    (B) 4

    (C) 6

    (D) 14

    (E) 30

19. $3 \int e^{3x}\, dx =$

    (A) $e^{-3x} + C$

    (B) $e^{-x} + C$

    (C) $e^{x} + C$

    (D) $e^{3x} + C$

    (E) $\frac{1}{3}e^{3x} + C$

20. $\int (x^2 + 2)\sqrt{x}\, dx =$

    (A) $x^2 + 4x^{\frac{3}{2}} + x + C$

    (B) $\frac{2}{7}x^{\frac{7}{2}} + \frac{4}{3}x^{\frac{3}{2}} + C$

    (C) $x^2 + x + C$

    (D) $\frac{2}{5}x^{\frac{5}{2}} + 2x^{\frac{1}{2}} + C$

    (E) $\frac{5}{2}\sqrt{x} + \frac{2}{\sqrt{x}} + c$

21. $\int_{0}^{2}(x^2 - 4x)e^{6x^2 - x^3}\, dx =$

    (A) $-\frac{e^{16}}{3}$

    (B) $\quad 0$

    (C) $\quad \frac{e^{16}}{3}$

    (D) $\quad \frac{1-e^{16}}{3}$

    (E) $\quad \frac{2-e^{16}}{3}$

22. $\int (\frac{2}{x^2} + \frac{1}{x} - 5\sqrt{x} + \frac{7}{\sqrt[3]{x^5}}) \, dx =$

23. $\int \frac{1}{x \ln x} \, dx =$

24. $\int 5^{\cot x} \csc^2 x \, dx =$

LEVEL 1: LIMITS AND CONTINUITY

25. $\lim_{x \to 7} \frac{2x^2 - 13x - 7}{x - 7} =$

    (A) -1

    (B)   0

    (C)   2

    (D)   15

    (E) ∞

26. If $h(x) = \frac{5x^2 - 3x + 2}{3x^2 - 2x}$, then $\lim_{x \to 1} h(x) =$

    (A) -1

    (B)   0

    (C) $\frac{5}{3}$

    (D) $\frac{7}{4}$

    (E)   4

27. $\lim_{x \to \infty} \frac{3x^2 - 2x + 1}{7x^2 + 5x - 3}$

    (A) $-\frac{1}{3}$

    (B)   0

    (C) $\frac{3}{7}$

    (D) $\frac{7}{3}$

    (E) ∞

28. If the function g is continuous for all real numbers and if $g(x) = \frac{x^2 - x - 6}{x - 3}$ for all $x \neq 3$, then $g(3) =$

    (A) 0

    (B) 1

    (C) 2

    (D) 5

    (E) $f(3)$ is not defined

29. $\lim_{x \to 0} \frac{\sin^3 5x}{x^3}$

    (A) -125

    (B) -5

    (C) 5

    (D) 125

    (E) The limit does not exist

30. $\lim_{x \to 0} \frac{3 \tan x - 3 \cos^2 x \tan x}{x^3}$

    (A) 0

    (B) $\frac{1}{3}$

    (C) 3

    (D) 27

    (E) ∞

31. If the function f is continuous for all x in the interval $[a, b]$, then at any point c in the interval (a, b), which of the following must be true?

    (A) $\lim_{x \to c} f(x) = f(c)$

    (B) $f'(c)$ exists

    (C) $f(c) = 0$

    (D) $f(c) = f(b) - f(a)$

    (E) $\frac{1}{b-a} \int_a^b f(x)\, dx = f(c)$

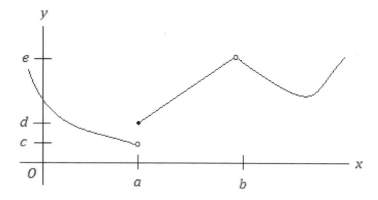

32. The graph of the function h is shown in the figure above. Which of the following statements about h is true?

    (A) $\lim_{x \to a} h(x) = c$
    (B) $\lim_{x \to a} h(x) = d$
    (C) $\lim_{x \to b} h(x) = e$
    (D) $\lim_{x \to b} h(x) = h(b)$
    (E) $\lim_{x \to b} h(x)$ does not exist

LEVEL 2: PRECALCULUS

33. If $g(f(x)) = \frac{5 \ln(2^x+1)-2}{\ln(2^x+1)+3}$ and $g(x) = \frac{5x-2}{x+3}$, then $f(x) =$

    (A) $\ln x$
    (B) $\ln 2^x$
    (C) $\ln(2^x + 1)$
    (D) $\ln x^2$
    (E) $\ln(x^2 + 1)$

34. Suppose that g is a function that is defined on $(-\infty, \infty)$. Which of the following conditions guarantees that g^{-1} exists?

    (A) g is symmetric with respect to the origin.
    (B) g is continuous at all real numbers.
    (C) g has no points of inflection.
    (D) g is a strictly decreasing function.
    (E) $g'(x) \neq 0$ for every real number x.

35. Let $g(x) = \sin(\arctan x)$. The range of g is

    (A) $\{x \mid -1 \leq x \leq 1\}$
    (B) $\{x \mid -1 < x < 1\}$
    (C) $\{x \mid 0 \leq x \leq 1\}$
    (D) $\{x \mid 0 \leq x < 1\}$
    (E) $\{x \mid -\frac{\pi}{2} < x < \frac{\pi}{2}\}$

36. If $\log_b\left(5^b\right) = \frac{b}{3}$, then $b =$

    (A) 125
    (B) 25
    (C) 5
    (D) 3
    (E) 1

37. What is the range of the following function?

$$T(x) = 2\cos(3x - 2\pi) - 5$$

    (A) $3 \leq y \leq 7$
    (B) $-3 \leq y \leq 7$
    (C) $-3 \leq y \leq 2$
    (D) $-7 \leq y \leq 2$
    (E) $-7 \leq y \leq -3$

38. * If $a(x) = \sqrt[5]{x^3 - 2}$, what is $a^{-1}(2.2)$?

    (A) 3.77
    (B) 4.23
    (C) 4.87
    (D) 5.01
    (E) 5.76

39. What is the period of the graph of $y = \frac{2}{3}\tan(\frac{5}{2}\pi\theta - 2)$?

    (A) $\frac{4}{15}$
    (B) $\frac{2}{5}$
    (C) $\frac{2}{3}$
    (D) $\frac{4\pi}{15}$
    (E) $\frac{2\pi}{5}$

20

40. If $\arcsin(\sin x) = \frac{\pi}{4}$ and $0 \le x \le 2\pi$, then x could equal

   (A) 0
   (B) $\frac{\pi}{6}$
   (C) $\frac{\pi}{3}$
   (D) $\frac{3\pi}{4}$
   (E) $\frac{5\pi}{4}$

LEVEL 2: DIFFERENTIATION

41. If $y = \sin^2 5x$, then $\frac{dy}{dx} =$

   (A) $2\sin 5x$
   (B) $10\sin 5x$
   (C) $2\cos 5x$
   (D) $2\sin 5x \cos 5x$
   (E) $10\sin 5x \cos 5x$

42. If $T(x) = \tan^2(5 - x)$, then $T'(0)$ is equal to which of the following?

   (A) $-2\tan 5 \sec 5$
   (B) $-2\tan 5 \sec^2 5$
   (C) $-2\tan^2 5 \sec 5$
   (D) $-2\tan^2 5 \sec^2 5$
   (E) $-2\sec^2 5$

21

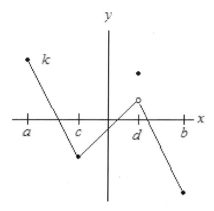

43. The function k, whose graph consists of three line segments, is shown above. Which of the following are true for k on the open interval (a, b) ?

    I. $\lim_{x \to c} k(x)$ exists.
    II. The domain of the derivative of k is the open interval (c, d).
    III. The derivative of k is negative on the interval (d, b).

    (A) I only
    (B) II only
    (C) III only
    (D) I and III only
    (E) II, and III only

44. If $f(x) = x\sqrt{3x + 5}$, then $f'(x) =$

    (A) $\dfrac{9}{2\sqrt{3x+5}}$

    (B) $\dfrac{x}{2\sqrt{3x+5}}$

    (C) $\dfrac{9x}{\sqrt{3x+5}}$

    (D) $\dfrac{9x}{2\sqrt{3x+5}}$

    (E) $\dfrac{9x+10}{2\sqrt{3x+5}}$

45. The slope of the tangent line to the curve $xy^5 - x^3y^4 = 10$ at $(-2, -1)$ is

    (A)   0

    (B) $-\dfrac{2}{7}$

    (C) $-\dfrac{13}{42}$

    (D) $-\dfrac{1}{3}$

    (E) $-\dfrac{5}{14}$

46. Let $f(x) = -3x^2 + x - 5$. A value of c that satisfies the conclusion of the Mean Value Theorem for f on the interval $[-2,2]$ is

    (A) -2

    (B) $-\dfrac{1}{2}$

    (C) $-\dfrac{1}{6}$

    (D) 0

    (E) $\dfrac{1}{2}$

47. If $g(x) = -x^5 + \dfrac{1}{x} - \sqrt[3]{x} + \dfrac{1}{\sqrt{x^5}}$, then $g'(1) =$

    (A) $-\dfrac{53}{6}$

    (B) $-\dfrac{58}{15}$

    (C)   0

    (D) $\dfrac{58}{15}$

    (E) $\dfrac{53}{6}$

48. The *derivative* of $g(x) = \frac{x^7}{7} - \frac{x^6}{5}$ attains its minimum value at $x =$

(A) $\frac{7}{5}$

(B) $\frac{6}{5}$

(C) 1

(D) 0

(E) -1

LEVEL 2: INTEGRATION

49. $\int_0^2 \frac{3x^2\,dx}{\sqrt{8-x^3}} =$

(A) $-4\sqrt{2}$
(B) $1 - 4\sqrt{2}$
(C) $4\sqrt{2} - 1$
(D) $4\sqrt{2}$
(E) $4\sqrt{2} + 1$

50. $\int_0^{\frac{\pi}{12}} \tan^2 3x\,dx =$

(A) $4 - \frac{\pi}{4}$

(B) $\sqrt{3} - \frac{1}{4}$

(C) $\frac{1}{3}$

(D) $\frac{12 - 3\pi}{4}$

(E) $\frac{4 - \pi}{12}$

51. $\int_1^3 \frac{x^2 + x - 1}{x^2}\,dx =$

(A) -3

(B) $\ln 3 - \frac{4}{3}$

(C) $\ln 3$

(D) $\frac{4}{3}$

(E) $\ln 3 + \frac{4}{3}$

52. The solution to the differential equation $\frac{dy}{dx} = \frac{x^2}{y^4}$, where $y(3) = 0$, is

(A) $y = \sqrt[5]{\frac{5}{3}x^3 - 45}$

(B) $y = \sqrt[5]{\frac{5}{3}x^3 - 9}$

(C) $y = \sqrt[5]{\frac{5}{3}x^3} - 45$

(D) $y = \sqrt[5]{\frac{5}{3}x^3} - \sqrt[5]{45}$

(E) $y = \sqrt[5]{\frac{5}{3}x^3}$

53. Each of the following is an antiderivative of $\frac{(\ln x)^2 - 2}{x}$ EXCEPT

(A) $\frac{(\ln x)^3}{3} - \ln x^2$

(B) $\frac{(\ln x)^3}{3} - \ln x^2 + 3$

(C) $\frac{(\ln x)^3}{3} - 2\ln|x|$

(D) $1 - \ln x^2 + \frac{(\ln x)^3}{3}$

(E) $\ln x - \ln x^2$

54. $\int \frac{8}{1+x^2} dx =$

(A) $8\ln(1 + x^2) + C$

(B) $8x - \frac{8}{x} + C$

(C) $8\tan^{-1} x + C$

(D) $\frac{4}{x}\ln(1 + x^2) + C$

(E) $-\frac{16x}{(1+x^2)^2}$

25

55. The area of the region bounded by the lines $x = 1$, $x = 4$, and $y = 0$ and the curve $y = e^{3x}$ is

    (A) $\frac{1}{3}e^3(e^9 - 1)$

    (B) $e^3(e^9 - 1)$

    (C) $e^{12} - 1$

    (D) $3e^3(e^9 - 1)$

    (E) $3e^{12}$

56. A population of protozoa is growing at a rate of $400e^{\frac{5t}{2}}$ protozoa per second. At $t = 0$ seconds, the number of protozoa present was 160. Find the number present after 2 seconds.

    (A) $320e^5$

    (B) $160e^5$

    (C) $160e^2$

    (D) $80e^2$

    (E) $e^{\frac{2}{5}}$

LEVEL 2: LIMITS AND CONTINUITY

57. What is $\lim_{h \to 0} \frac{\tan\left(\frac{\pi}{4}+h\right)-\tan\left(\frac{\pi}{4}\right)}{h}$?

    (A) 0

    (B) $\frac{1}{2}$

    (C) 1

    (D) 2

    (E) The limit does not exist.

58. What is $\lim_{x \to \infty} \frac{5-x^2+3x^3}{x^3-2x+3}$?

    (A) 1

    (B) $\frac{5}{3}$

    (C) 3

    (D) 1

    (E) The limit does not exist.

59. $\lim_{h \to 0} \frac{1}{h} \ln(\frac{10+h}{10})$ is equal to

(A) $\frac{1}{10}$

(B) 0

(C) 10

(D) e^{10}

(E) The limit does not exist.

60. Let the function f be defined by $f(x) = \begin{cases} \frac{\tan x}{x}, & \text{for } x \neq 0. \\ 0, & \text{for } x = 0. \end{cases}$
    Which of the following are true about f?

    I. $\lim_{x \to 0} f(x)$ exists.
    II. $f(0)$ exists.
    III. f is continuous at $x = 0$.

    (A) None
    (B) I only
    (C) II only
    (D) I and II only
    (E) I, II, and III

61. Let the function k satisfy $\lim_{h \to 0} \frac{k(7+h)-k(7)}{h} = 12$. Which of the
    following must be true ?

    I. k is continuous at $x = 7$
    II. $k'(7)$ exists
    III. k' is continuous at $x = 7$

    (A) None
    (B) I only
    (C) II only
    (D) I and II only
    (E) I, II, and III

62. $\lim_{x \to 0} \frac{\sin 7x}{\sin 4x} =$

63. $\lim_{x \to 11} \frac{x}{(x-11)^2} =$

27

64. Let f be the function defined by

$$f(x) = \begin{cases} \dfrac{5e^{x-7}}{1 + \ln|x-8|}, & x \leq 7 \\ \dfrac{15\cos(x-7)}{\sin(7-x)+3}, & x > 7 \end{cases}$$

Show that f is continuous at $x = 7$.

LEVEL 3: PRECALCULUS

65. Let $t(x) = |\cos(x) + \frac{3}{2}|$. The minimum value attained by t is

(A) $-\dfrac{5}{2}$

(B) $-\dfrac{3}{2}$

(C) 0

(D) $\dfrac{1}{2}$

(E) $\dfrac{3}{2}$

66. For what value of k will the graphs of $y = 3x + k$ and $y^2 = 6x$ intersect in exactly one point?

67. Let $f(x) = 2x^3 - x^2 + 3x$ and $g(x) = x^3 + 4x^2 - 1$. Find the x-coordinates of all points common to the graphs of f and g.

68. Find the domain of $k\,(x) = \dfrac{1}{\sqrt{x^2-4x-5}}$.

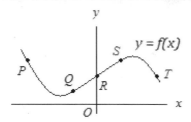

69. At which of the five points on the graph in the figure above is $\frac{dy}{dx}$ negative and $\frac{d^2y}{dx^2}$ positive?

    (A) P
    (B) Q
    (C) R
    (D) S
    (E) T

70. Given the function defined by $f(x) = 5x^3 - 3x^5$, find all values of x for which the graph of f is concave down.

    (A) $-\frac{\sqrt{2}}{2} < x < \frac{\sqrt{2}}{2}$
    (B) $x > \frac{\sqrt{2}}{2}$
    (C) $-\frac{1}{2} < x < 0$ or $x > \frac{1}{2}$
    (D) $-\frac{\sqrt{2}}{2} < x < 0$ or $x > \frac{\sqrt{2}}{2}$
    (E) $x < 0$

71. If the line $7x - 4y = 3$ is tangent in the first quadrant to the curve $y = x^3 + x + c$, then c is

    (A) $-\frac{1}{2}$
    (B) $-\frac{1}{4}$
    (C) 0
    (D) $\frac{1}{4}$
    (E) $\frac{1}{2}$

29

72. Which of the following statements about the function given by $g(x) = x^6 + 4x^5$ is true?

   (A) The function has two relative extrema and the graph of the function has two points of inflection.
   (B) The function has one relative extremum and the graph of the function has two points of inflection
   (C) The function has two relative extrema and the graph of the function has one point of inflection.
   (D) The function has one relative extremum and the graph of the function has one point of inflection.
   (E) The function has no relative extrema.

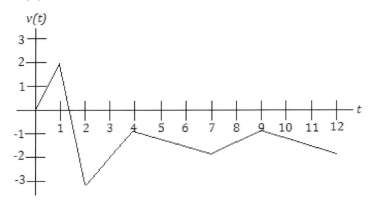

73. A fly is walking along a straight piece of string. The velocity $v(t)$ of the fly at time t, $0 \le t \le 12$, is given in the graph above. According to the graph, at what time t is the speed of the fly greatest?

   (A) 1
   (B) 1.4
   (C) 2
   (D) 4
   (E) 7

74. If $g(x) = x^{\frac{1}{3}}(x + 3)^{\frac{1}{2}}$ for all x, then the domain of g' is

   (A) $\{x | x$ is a real number$\}$
   (B) $\{x | x \ne 0\}$
   (C) $\{x | x \ne 0$ and $x \ne 2\}$
   (D) $\{x | x > -3$ and $x \ne 0\}$
   (E) $\{x | -3 < x < 0\}$

30

75. $\frac{d}{dx}[\sin^{-1}(\frac{x}{2})] =$

(A) $-\frac{1}{\sqrt{4-x^2}}$

(B) $\frac{1}{\sqrt{4-x^2}}$

(C) $-\frac{1}{2\sqrt{1-x^2}}$

(D) $\frac{1}{2\sqrt{1-x^2}}$

(E) $\frac{1}{\sqrt{1-4x^2}}$

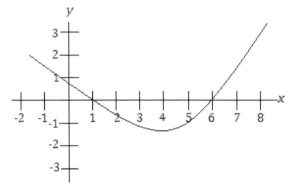

76. The **derivative** of g is graphed above. Give a value of x where g has a local minimum.

(A) 0
(B) 1
(C) 4
(D) 6
(E) There is no such value of x.

77. If $\sec(x^2 y) = y$, then $\frac{dy}{dx} =$

(A) $\frac{-2y\sec(x^2 y)}{1-x\sec(x^2 y)}$

(B) $\frac{2xy\tan(x^2 y)}{\cos(x^2 y)-x^2\tan(x^2 y)}$

(C) $\frac{1}{\sec(x^2 y)\tan(x^2 y)}$

(D) $\frac{1-y\tan^2(x^2 y)}{x\tan^2(x^2 y)}$

(E) $\tan^2(x^2 y)$

78. A point moves in a straight line so that its distance at time t from a fixed point of the line is $2t^3 - 9t^2 + 12t$. The *total* distance that the point travels from $t = 0$ to $t = 4$ is

   (A) 32
   (B) 33
   (C) 34
   (D) 35
   (E) 36

79. * Two particles start at the origin and move along the x-axis. For $0 \le t \le 10$, their position functions are given by $x = \cos t$ and $y = \ln(2t) + 1$. For how many values of t do the particles have the same velocity?

   (A) None
   (B) One
   (C) Two
   (D) Three
   (E) Four

80. Consider the equation $x^2 + e^{xy} + y^2 = 2$. Find $\frac{d^2y}{dx^2}$ at $(0,1)$.

LEVEL 3: INTEGRATION

81. The area of the region in the first quadrant bounded by the graph of $y = x^2\sqrt{1 - x^3}$, the line $x = 1$, and the x-axis is

   (A) $\frac{2}{9}$

   (B) $\frac{2\sqrt{2}}{9}$

   (C) $\frac{2\sqrt{3}}{9}$

   (D) $\frac{4}{9}$

   (E) $\frac{16}{9}$

82. A particle moves in a straight line with velocity $v(t) = t - \sqrt{t}$ beginning at time $t = 0$. How far is the particle from its starting point at time $t = 4$?

   (A) 0

   (B) 2

   (C) $\frac{8}{3}$

   (D) $\frac{40}{3}$

   (E) 20

83. The acceleration $a(t)$ of a body moving in a straight line is given in terms of time t by $a(t) = 3 - 2t$. If the velocity of the body is 10 at $t = 1$ and if $s(t)$ is the distance of the body from the origin at time t, then $s(5) - s(1) =$

   (A) $\frac{10}{3}$

   (B) $\frac{20}{3}$

   (C) $\frac{40}{3}$

   (D) $\frac{80}{3}$

   (E) $\frac{100}{3}$

84. The area of the region completely bounded by the curve $y = -x^2 + 2x + 5$ and the line $y = 2$ is

   (A) $\frac{4}{3}$

   (B) $\frac{8}{3}$

   (C) $\frac{16}{3}$

   (D) $\frac{24}{3}$

   (E) $\frac{32}{3}$

85. Let f and g be continuous functions such that $f'(x) = g(x)$ for all x. It follows that $\int_a^b g(x)dx =$

   (A) $f(a) - f(b)$
   (B) $f(b) - f(a)$
   (C) $f'(a) - f'(b)$
   (D) $f'(b) - f'(a)$
   (E) $f''(b) - f''(a)$

86. If $\frac{dy}{dx} = xy + 3y$ and if $y = 5$ when $x = 0$, then $y =$

   (A) $5e^{x^2+3x}$
   (B) e^{x^2+3x}
   (C) $5 + e^{x^2+3x}$
   (D) $4 + e^{x^2+3x}$
   (E) $3x^2 + 4$

87. The average value of $\frac{1}{\sqrt{x}}$ over the interval $1 \le x \le 4$ is

   (A) $-\frac{1}{2}$
   (B) 0
   (C) $\frac{1}{2}$
   (D) $\frac{2}{3}$
   (E) 2

88. Given $h(x) = \begin{cases} \sin \pi x & \text{for } x < 0 \\ x^2 - x & \text{for } x \ge 0 \end{cases}$, we have $\int_{-2}^{1} h(x)dx =$

   (A) $-\frac{1}{6} - \frac{1}{\pi}$
   (B) $-\frac{1}{6}$
   (C) $\frac{1}{6} - \frac{1}{\pi}$
   (D) $\frac{1}{6}$
   (E) $\frac{1}{6} + \frac{1}{\pi}$

34

89. If $\int_j^k f(x)dx = k^2 - j^2$, then $\int_j^k (3f(x) - 2x)dx =$

(A) $k^2 - j^2$
(B) $2k^2 - 2j^2$
(C) $2j^2 - 2k^2$
(D) $3k^2 - 3j^2$
(E) $3j^2 - 3k^2$

90. If $\int_2^5 f(3x + k)dx = b$ where k and b are real numbers, then $\int_{6+k}^{15+k} f(x)dx =$

(A) $3b$

(B) b

(C) $\frac{b}{3}$

(D) $3b + k$

(E) $b + k$

91. * Calculate the approximate area under the curve $f(x) = x^2$ and bounded by the lines $x = 2$ and $x = 3$ by the trapezoidal rule, using three equal subintervals.

(A) 1.285
(B) 3.176
(C) 6.352
(D) 8.596
(E) 12.704

92. A point moves in a straight line so that its velocity at time t is $2t^3 - 5t^2 + 2t$. What is the *total* distance that the point travels from $t = 0$ to $t = 3$?

93. If $\lim_{x \to c} f(x) = f(\lim_{x \to c} x)$ for all c in the interval (a, b), which of the following *must* be true?

    (A) f is continuous on (a, b).

    (B) f is differentiable on (a, b).

    (C) f is a polynomial.

    (D) $f'(x) = 0$ for some $x \in (a, b)$.

    (E) If $f(c)$ is a minimum of f, then $f'(c) = 0$.

94. Let f be defined by $f(x) = \dfrac{1}{\sqrt{17-x^2}} + \sqrt{x-3}$ for $-2 \leq x \leq 10$.
Let g be defined by $g(x) = \begin{cases} f(x) + 2 & \text{for } -2 \leq x \leq 4 \\ |x - 8| & \text{for } 4 < x \leq 10 \end{cases}$.
Is g continuous at $x = 4$? Use the definition of continuity to explain your answer.

95. A 5000 gallon tank is filled to capacity with water. At time $t = 0$, water begins to leak out of the tank at a rate modeled by $R(t)$, measured in gallons per hour, where

$$R(t) = \begin{cases} \dfrac{300t}{t+1}, & 0 \leq t \leq 4 \\ 500e^{-0.5t}, & t > 4 \end{cases}$$

Is R continuous at $t = 4$? Show the work that leads to your answer.

96. The function $g(x) = \dfrac{x^2 + 4x - 12}{x^2 + 3x - 10}$ has a removable discontinuity at $x = c$. Find c, and define a function G such that G is continuous at $x = c$ and $G(x) = g(x)$ for all x in the domain of g.

97. Suppose that f is an even function (so that $f(-x) = f(x)$ for all x), and that $f'(c)$ exists. Then $f'(-c)$ must be equal to

(A) $f'(c)$

(B) $-f'(c)$

(C) $\dfrac{1}{f'(c)}$

(D) $-\dfrac{1}{f'(c)}$

(E) $f'(1-c)$

98. The function $g(x) = 10x^4 - 7e^{x-1}$, $x > \frac{1}{2}$ is invertible. The derivative of g^{-1} at $x = 3$ is

(A) $-\dfrac{7}{e}$

(B) $-\dfrac{e}{7}$

(C) 1

(D) $\dfrac{1}{33}$

(E) 33

99. The radius of a spherical balloon is decreasing at a constant rate of 0.5 centimeters per second. At the instant when the volume V becomes 288π cubic centimeters, what is the rate of decrease, in square centimeters per second, of the surface area of the balloon?

(A) 24π
(B) 48π
(C) 64π
(D) 72π
(E) 96π

100. If $y = e^{kx}$, then $\frac{d^n y}{dx^n} =$

(A) $n!\, e^{kx}$
(B) $n^n e^{kx}$
(C) $n^k e^{kx}$
(D) $k^n e^{kx}$
(E) $n e^{kx}$

101. For small values of h, the function $\frac{1}{\sqrt[3]{27+h}}$ is best approximated by

(A) $\frac{3-h}{27}$

(B) $\frac{27-h}{81}$

(C) $\frac{81-h}{81}$

(D) $\frac{27-h}{243}$

(E) $\frac{81-h}{243}$

x	2.5	2.6	2.7	2.8
$f(x)$	7	7.4	7.7	7.9

102. Let f be a function that is concave down for all x in the closed interval $[2,3]$, with selected values shown in the above table. Which of the following inequalities must be true?

(A) $f'(2.7) > 3$
(B) $2 < f'(2.7) < 3$
(C) $1 < f'(2.7) < 2$
(D) $0 < f'(2.7) < 1$
(E) $f'(2.7) < 0$

103. Consider the differential equation $\frac{dy}{dx} = e^{y-1}(2x^3 - 5)$. Let $y = f(x)$ be the particular solution to the differential equation that passes through $(1,1)$. Write an equation for the line tangent to the graph of f at the point $(1,1)$, and use the tangent line to approximate $f(1.1)$.

38

t (minutes)	0	1	2	3	4
$G(t)$ (pints)	0	2.2	4.5	6.8	8.3

104. Gasoline is dripping out of a gas pump, filling up a bucket. The amount of gasoline in the bucket at time t, $0 \leq t \leq 4$, is given by a differentiable function G, where t is measured in minutes. Selected values of $G(t)$, measured in pints, are given in the table above. Is there a time t, $1 \leq t \leq 3$, at which $G'(t) = 2.3$? Justify your answer.

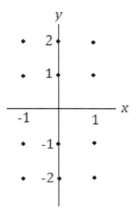

105. Consider the differential equation $\frac{dy}{dx} = -\frac{x^2}{y}$. On the axes provided above, sketch a slope field for the differential equation at the twelve points indicated.

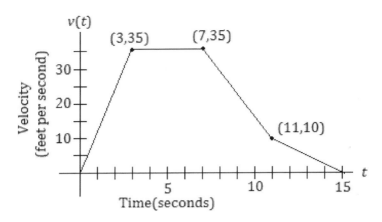

106. A bus is traveling on a straight road. For $0 \le t \le 15$ seconds, the bus's velocity $v(t)$, in feet per second, is modeled by the function shown in the graph above. For each of $v'(3)$, $v'(8)$, and $v'(11)$, find the value or explain why it does not exist. Indicate units of measure.

107. Two particles are moving along the x-axis. For $0 \le t \le 10$, the position of particle A at time t is given by $a(t) = 3\sin t$, and the position of particle B at time t is given by $b(t) = t^3 - 12t^2 + 21t - 1$. For $0 \le t \le 10$, find all times t during which the two particles travel in opposite directions.

x	0	$0 < x < 1$	1	$1 < x < 2$	2	$2 < x < 3$	3
$f(x)$	-4	$-$	-3	$-$	-1	$-$	-2
$f'(x)$	3	$+$	0	$+$	0	$-$	-5

108. The differentiable function f is defined for all real numbers x. Values of f and f' for various values of x are given in the table above. Find the x-coordinate of each relative maximum of f on the interval $[0,3]$. Justify your answers.

109. Consider a differentiable function g with domain all positive real numbers, satisfying $g'(x) = \frac{2-x}{x^3}$ for $x > 0$. Find the x-coordinates of all relative minima and maxima, find all intervals on which the graph of g is concave up, and find all intervals on which the graph of g is concave down. Justify your answers.

40

t (minutes)	0	1	2	3	4
$G(t)$ (pints)	0	2.2	4.5	6.8	8.3

110. Gasoline is dripping out of a gas pump, filling up a bucket. The amount of gasoline in the bucket at time t, $0 \leq t \leq 4$, is given by a differentiable function G, where t is measured in minutes. Selected values of $G(t)$, measured in pints, are given in the table above. Use the data in the table to approximate $G'(1.5)$. Show the computations that lead to your answer, and indicate units of measure.

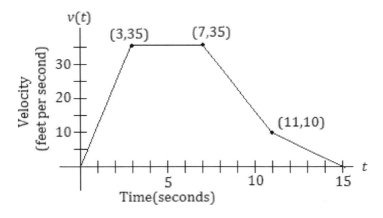

111. A bus is traveling on a straight road. For $0 \leq t \leq 15$ seconds, the bus's velocity $v(t)$, in feet per second, is modeled by the function defined by the graph above. Let $a(t)$ be the bus's acceleration at time t, in feet per second per second. For $0 < t < 15$, write a piecewise-defined function for $a(t)$.

x	0	$0 < x < 1$	1	$1 < x < 2$	2	$2 < x < 3$	3
$f(x)$	5	+	2	+	3	+	0
$f'(x)$	-2	$-$	0	+	0	$-$	-8

112. The twice-differentiable function f is defined for all real numbers x. Values of f and f' for various values of x are given in the table above. Explain why there must be a value c, for $0 < c < 3$, such that $f''(c) = -2$.

41

113. The region in the xy-plane bounded by the graph of $y = \dfrac{\ln(x)}{\sqrt{x}}$, $x = 1$, $x = 4$, and the x-axis is rotated about the x-axis. What is the volume of the solid generated?

   (A) $\dfrac{(\ln 4)^3}{3} - 1$

   (B) $\dfrac{\pi (\ln 4)^3}{3} - 1$

   (C) $\dfrac{\pi (\ln 4)^3 - 1}{3}$

   (D) $\dfrac{\pi (\ln 4)^3}{3}$

   (E) $\dfrac{\pi (\ln 4)^3}{3} + 1$

114. * Water is leaking from an air conditioning unit at the rate of $f(t) = 750e^{-\frac{t}{3}}$ quarts per hour, where t is measured in hours. Approximately how much water has leaked out of the unit after 5 hours?

   (A) 47
   (B) 142
   (C) 608
   (D) 1825
   (E) 2250

115. * The average value of $(\ln x)^5$ on the interval $[2,5]$ is

   (A) 0.584
   (B) 1.299
   (C) 3.896
   (D) 11.687
   (E) 35.060

116. * If $f'(x) = \cos(\frac{\ln(x+1)}{4})$ and $f(0) = 2$, then $f(3) =$

   (A)   4.919
   (B)   2.919
   (C) -0.75
   (D) -1.5
   (E) -3

42

117. * Let D be the region enclosed by $y = \sin x$ and $y = \cos x$ for $0 \le x \le \frac{\pi}{4}$. The volume of the solid generated when D is revolved around the line $x = 4$ is

(A) 0.696
(B) 0.897
(C) 1.793
(D) 4.857
(E) 9.715

118. * Let the function F be defined by $F(x) = \int_0^x \cos(u^4)\, du$ on the closed interval $[0,1.5]$. F has a local maximum at $x =$

(A) 0
(B) 1.120
(C) 1.571
(D) 1.473
(E) 2

119. The expression $\frac{1}{100}\left(\sqrt[3]{\frac{1}{100}} + \sqrt[3]{\frac{2}{100}} + \sqrt[3]{\frac{3}{100}} + \cdots + \sqrt[3]{\frac{100}{100}}\right)$ is a Riemann sum approximation for

(A) $\frac{1}{100}\int_0^{100} \sqrt[3]{x}\, dx$

(B) $\frac{1}{100}\int_0^1 \sqrt[3]{x}\, dx$

(C) $\frac{1}{100}\int_0^1 \sqrt[3]{\frac{x}{100}}\, dx$

(D) $\int_0^1 \sqrt[3]{x}\, dx$

(E) $\int_0^1 \sqrt[3]{\frac{x}{100}}\, dx$

t (minutes)	0	1	2	3	4
$G(t)$ (pints)	0	2.2	4.5	6.8	8.3

120. Gasoline is dripping out of a gas pump, filling up a bucket. The amount of gasoline in the bucket at time t, $0 \leq t \leq 4$, is given by a continuous function G, where t is measured in minutes. Selected values of $G(t)$, measured in pints, are given in the table above. Use a midpoint sum with two subintervals of equal length indicated by the given data to approximate $\frac{1}{4}\int_0^4 G(t)\, dt$. Using correct units, explain the meaning of $\frac{1}{4}\int_0^4 G(t)\, dt$ in the context of the problem.

121. Consider the differential equation $\frac{dy}{dx} = e^{y-1}(2x^3 - 5)$. Let $y = f(x)$ be the particular solution to the differential equation that passes through $(1,1)$. Find $y = f(x)$.

x	0	1	2	3
$f(x)$	2	7	−1	1
$f'(x)$	3	0	0	−5
$g(x)$	−2	−5	−2	4
$g'(x)$	8	9	−6	0

122. The differentiable functions f and g are defined for all real numbers x. Values of f, f', g, and g' for various values of x are given in the table above. Evaluate $\int_0^3 g'(f(x))f'(x)\, dx$.

44

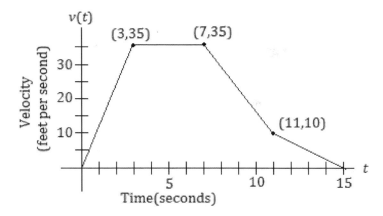

123. A bus is traveling on a straight road. For $0 \le t \le 15$ seconds, the bus's velocity $v(t)$, in feet per second, is modeled by the function defined by the graph above. Find $\int_0^{15} v(t)\, dt$. Using correct units, explain the meaning of $\int_0^{15} v(t)\, dt$.

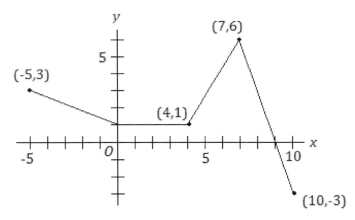

124. The function g is defined on the closed interval $[-5,10]$. The graph of g consists of four line segments and is shown in the figure above. Let G be defined by $G(x) = \int_0^x g(x)\, dx$. Compute $\dfrac{G(-5)+G(4)}{G(10)-G(7)}$.

125. * A 5000 gallon tank is filled to capacity with water. At time $t = 0$, water begins to leak out of the tank at a rate modeled by $R(t)$, measured in gallons per hour, where

$$R(t) = \begin{cases} \dfrac{300t}{t+1}, & 0 \le t \le 4 \\ 500e^{-0.5t}, & t > 4 \end{cases}$$

Find the average rate at which water is leaking from the tank between time $t = 0$ and time $t = 10$ hours. Then write, but do not solve, an equation involving an integral to find the time T when the amount of water in the tank is 1000 gallons.

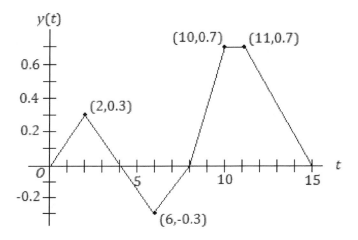

126. Joe is driving his car along a straight road. For $0 \le t \le 15$ seconds, his velocity $v(t)$, in miles per minute, is modeled by the function defined by the graph above. Using correct units, explain the meaning of $\int_0^{15} |v(t)| \, dt$ in terms of Joe's trip. Then find the value of $\int_0^{15} |v(t)| \, dt$.

x	1	5	6	8	11
$f(x)$	3	5	1	-3	4

127. Let f be a function that is continuous for all real numbers. The table above gives values of f for selected points in the closed interval $[1,11]$. Use a left Riemann Sum with subintervals indicated by the data in the table to approximate $\int_1^{11} f(x) \, dx$. Show the work that leads to your answer.

128. * Let R be the region in the first and second quadrants bounded above by the graph of $y = \frac{48}{2+x^4}$ and below by the horizontal line $y = 4$. The region R is the base of a solid whose cross sections perpendicular to the x-axis are semicircles. Find the volume of this solid.

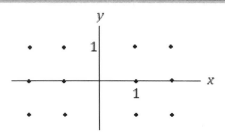

129 – 132 Consider the differential equation $\frac{dy}{dx} = \frac{y+1}{x}$ and the figure above.

129. On the axes provided, sketch a slope field for the differential equation at the twelve points indicated, and for $y > -1$, sketch the solution curve passing through the point $(-1,0)$. Then describe all points in the xy-plane, $x \neq 0$, for which $\frac{dy}{dx} = -1$.

130. Write an equation for the line tangent to the solution curve at the point $(-2,0)$. Use the equation to approximate $f(-1.5)$ where $y = f(x)$ is the particular solution of the differential equation with initial condition $f(-2) = 0$.

131. Find $y = f(x)$, the particular solution to the differential equation with the initial condition $f(-2) = 0$.

132. Describe the region in the xy-plane in which all solution curves to the differential equation are concave down.

133 – 136 * Suppose that the average annual salary of an NBA player is modeled by the function $S(t) = 161.4(1.169^t)$, where $S(t)$ is measured in thousands of dollars and t is measured in years since 1980 (for example, since $S(0) = 161.4$, the average salary of an NBA player in 1980 was \$161,400).

133. * Find the average rate of change of $S(t)$ over the interval $0 \le t \le 20$. Interpret this answer and indicate units of measure.

134. * Find the value of $S'(10)$. Using correct units, interpret the meaning of the value in the context of the problem.

135. * Use a right Riemann sum with five equal subintervals to approximate $\frac{1}{20}\int_0^{20} S(t)dt$. Does this approximation overestimate or underestimate the average salary from the beginning of 1980 through the end of 2000? Explain your reasoning.

136. * Find the year in which it occurs that the average annual salary is equal to the average salary from the beginning of 1980 through the end of 2000.

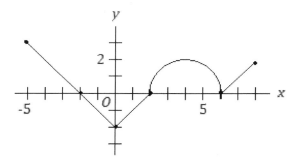

137 – 144 Let f be the continuous function defined on $[-5,8]$ whose graph, consisting of three line segments and a semicircle centered at $(4,0)$, is shown above. Let F be the function that is defined by $F(x) = \int_2^x f(t)\, dt$.

137. Find the values of $F(8)$ and $F(-1)$.

138. For each of $F'(-4)$, $F''(-4)$, $F'(6)$, and $F''(6)$, find the value or explain why it does not exist.

139. On what open intervals contained in $-5 < x < 8$ is the graph of F both increasing and concave up? Justify your answer.

140. Find the x-coordinate of each point at which the graph of F has a horizontal tangent line. For each of these points, determine whether F has a relative minimum, relative maximum, or neither a minimum nor a maximum at the point. Justify your answer.

48

141. For $-5 < x < 8$, find all values of x for which the graph of F has a point of inflection. Explain your reasoning.

142. Find the absolute minimum and absolute maximum of F over the closed interval $[-5,8]$. Explain your reasoning.

143. The function G is defined by $G(x) = \ln\frac{F(x)}{2x}$. Find $G'(-4)$.

144. The function H is defined by $H(x) = f\left(\frac{3x^2-2x}{e^{x-1}}\right)$. Find an equation of the tangent line to the graph of H at the point where $x = 1$.

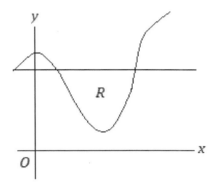

145 – 148 * Let R be the region in the first quadrant enclosed by the graph of $f(x) = x^6 - 3.5x^4 + 7$ and the horizontal line $y = 5$, as shown in the figure above.

145. * Write an equation for the tangent line to the graph of f at $x = -0.5$.

146. * Find the volume of the solid generated when R is rotated about the horizontal line $y = -3$.

147. * The region R is the base of a solid. For this solid, each cross section perpendicular to the x-axis is an equilateral triangle. Find the volume of the solid.

148. The vertical line $x = a$ divides R into two regions with equal areas. Write, but do not solve, an equation involving integral expressions whose solution gives the value a.

149 – 152 Let h and k be twice-differentiable functions such that $h(1) = -4$, $h(8) = 6$, $k(-3) = 1$, and $k(2) = 8$. Let f be the function given by $f(x) = h(k(x))$.

149. Let b satisfy $-4 < b < 6$. Explain why there must be a value a for $-3 < a < 2$ such that $f(a) = b$.

150. Is there a value c for $-3 < c < 2$ such that $f'(c) = 2$. Justify your answer.

151. Suppose that $h'(1) = k'(2)$ and $h'(8) = k'(-3)$. Explain why there must be a value d, with $-3 < d < 2$ such that $f''(d) = 0$.

152. Suppose that $h''(x) = k''(x) = 0$ for all x. Find all points of inflection on the graph of f.

153 – 160 * A particle moves along the x-axis so that its velocity v at time $t \geq 0$ is given by $v(t) = \cos(t^2)$. The position of the particle at time t is $s(t)$ and its position at time $t = 0$ is $s(0) = 2$.

153. * Find the acceleration of the particle at time $t = 4$. Is the speed of the particle increasing or decreasing at time $t = 4$? Justify your answer.

154. * Find all values of t in the interval $0 \leq t \leq 2$ for which the speed of the particle is $\frac{1}{2}$. For each such value of t determine if the particle is moving to the right or to the left.

155. * Find the total distance traveled by the particle from time $t = 0$ to $t = 2$.

156. * Find the position of the particle at time $t = 4$.

157. * Find all times t in the interval $0 \leq t \leq 3$ at which the particle changes direction. Justify your answer.

158. Determine all values $t \geq 0$ for which the acceleration is 0. Then determine all values of t, $0 \leq t \leq 3$, for which the particle is speeding up.

159. * For $0 \leq t \leq 3$, find the time t at which the particle is farthest to the right. Explain your answer.

160. * Find the value of the constant B for which $v(t)$ satisfies $Ba(t)\cos(t^2) - 2tv(t)\sin(t^2) = 0$, where $a(t)$ is the acceleration of the particle at time t.

50

Answers to
Calculus AB Problems

Level 1: Precalculus

1. A
2. A
3. E
4. B
5. D
6. C
7. A
8. D

Level 1: Differentiation

9. B
10. A
11. E
12. D
13. D
14. $-\dfrac{2}{3\sqrt[3]{x^5}} + (\ln 11)11^x$
15. $x^{\cos x}\left[\dfrac{\cos x - x\,(\ln x)(\sin x)}{x}\right]$
16. $f'(x) = \dfrac{-6x(\csc^2 3x)e^{\cot 3x} - e^{\cot 3x}}{2x\sqrt{x}}$

Level 1: Integration

17. E
18. C
19. D
20. B
21. D
22. $-\dfrac{2}{x} + \ln|x| - \dfrac{10}{3}\sqrt{x^3} - \dfrac{21}{2\sqrt[3]{x^2}} + C$

51

23. $\ln|\ln x| + C$

24. $-\dfrac{5^{\cot x}}{\ln 5} + C$

LEVEL 1: LIMITS AND CONTINUITY

25. D
26. E
27. C
28. D
29. D
30. C
31. A
32. C

LEVEL 2: PRECALCULUS

33. C
34. D
35. B
36. A
37. E
38. A
39. B
40. D

LEVEL 2: DIFFERENTIATION

41. E
42. B
43. D
44. E
45. C
46. D
47. A
48. C

LEVEL 2: INTEGRATION

49. D
50. E
51. E
52. A
53. E
54. C
55. A
56. B

LEVEL 2: LIMITS AND CONTINUITY

57. D
58. C
59. A
60. D
61. D
62. $\dfrac{7}{4}$
63. $+\infty$
64. $\lim_{x \to 7^-} f(x) = \dfrac{5e^{7-7}}{1+\ln|7-8|} = \dfrac{5e^0}{1+\ln 1} = \dfrac{5}{1+0} = 5$

$\lim_{x \to 7^+} f(x) = \dfrac{15\cos(7-7)}{\sin(7-7)+3} = \dfrac{15\cos 0}{\sin 0+3} = \dfrac{15(1)}{0+3} = \dfrac{15}{3} = 5$

So $\lim_{x \to 7} f(x) = 5$

Also, $f(7) = \dfrac{5e^{7-7}}{1+\ln|7-8|} = 5$. So, $\lim_{x \to 7} f(x) = f(7)$

It follows that f is continuous at $x = 7$

LEVEL 3: PRECALCULUS

65. D
66. $\dfrac{1}{2}$ or .5
67. $1, 2 + \sqrt{5}$, and $2 - \sqrt{5}$
68. $(-\infty, -1) \cup (5, \infty)$

LEVEL 3: DIFFERENTIATION

69. A
70. D
71. A
72. B
73. C
74. D
75. B
76. D
77. B
78. C
79. D
80. $-\frac{5}{4}$

LEVEL 3: INTEGRATION

81. A
82. C
83. D
84. E
85. B
86. A
87. D
88. B
89. B
90. A
91. C
92. $\frac{117}{16}$, 7.312 or 7.313

LEVEL 3: LIMITS AND CONTINUITY

93. A
94. $\lim_{x \to 4^-} g(x) = f(4) + 2 = 4$

$\lim_{x \to 4^+} g(x) = |4 - 8| = |-4| = 4$ _So $\lim_{x \to 4} g(x) = 4$.

Also, $g(4) = f(4) + 2 = 4$. So, $\lim_{x \to 4} g(x) = g(4)$.

It follows that g is continuous at $x = 4$.

95. $\lim_{t \to 4^-} R(t) = \frac{300(4)}{4+1} = 240$

$\lim_{t \to 4^+} R(t) = 500e^{-0.5(4)} = 500e^{-2}$

Since $\lim_{t \to 4^-} R(t) \neq \lim_{t \to 4^+} r(t)$, $\lim_{t \to 4} R(t)$ does not exist.

It follows that R is *not* continuous at $t = 4$.

96. $c = 2$

$$G(x) = \begin{cases} \frac{x^2+4x-12}{x^2+3x-10}, & x \neq 2 \\ \frac{8}{7}, & x = 2 \end{cases}$$

LEVEL 4: DIFFERENTIATION

97. B
98. D
99. A
100. D
101. E
102. B
103. $y - 1 = -3(x - 1)$.

$f(1.1) \approx .7$.

104. Since G is differentiable, it follows that G is continuous on [1,3]. We have $\frac{G(3)-G(1)}{3-1} = \frac{6.8-2.2}{2} = 2.3$. By the Mean Value Theorem, there is at least one time t, $1 < t < 3$, for which $G'(t) = 2.3$.

105.

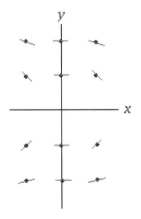

106. $\lim_{x\to 3^-}\left(\frac{v(t)-v(3)}{t-3}\right)=\frac{35}{3}$ and $\lim_{x\to 3^+}\left(\frac{v(t)-v(3)}{t-3}\right)=0$.

Since $\lim_{x\to 3^-}\left(\frac{v(t)-v(3)}{t-3}\right)\neq\lim_{x\to 3^+}\left(\frac{v(t)-v(3)}{t-3}\right)$, $v'(3)$ does not exist.

$v'(8)=\frac{10-35}{11-7}=-\frac{25}{4}$ ft/sec^2.

$\lim_{x\to 11^-}\left(\frac{v(t)-v(11)}{t-11}\right)=-\frac{25}{4}$

$\lim_{x\to 11^+}\left(\frac{v(t)-v(11)}{t-11}\right)=\frac{-10}{4}=-\frac{5}{2}$.

Since $\lim_{x\to 11^-}\left(\frac{v(t)-v(3)}{t-3}\right)\neq\lim_{x\to 11^+}\left(\frac{v(t)-v(3)}{t-3}\right)$, $v'(11)$ does not exist.

107. $\left(1,\frac{\pi}{2}\right)\cup\left(\frac{3\pi}{2},7\right)\cup(\frac{5\pi}{2},10]$.

108. The critical numbers of f are $x=1$ and $x=2$. But $x=2$ is the only critical number at which f' changes sign from positive to negative. Therefore $x=2$ is the only x-coordinate where f has a relative maximum.

109. $g'(x)=0$ at $x=2$, $g'(x)>0$ for $0<x<2$, and $g'(x)<0$ for $x>2$. It follows that g has a relative maximum at $x=2$.

$g''(x)=\frac{x^3(-1)-(2-x)\cdot 3x^2}{x^6}=\frac{x^2[-x-3(2-x)]}{x^6}=\frac{2(x-3)}{x^4}$.

$g''(x)=0$ at $x=3$.

$g''(x)<0$ for $0<x<3$, and $g''(x)>0$ for $x>3$.

So the graph of graph of g is concave down for $0<x<3$ and the graph of g is concave up for $x>3$.

110. $G'(1.5)\approx\frac{G(2)-G(1)}{2-1}=\frac{4.5-2.2}{1}=2.3$ pints/minute.

111. $a(t)=\begin{cases} \frac{35}{3} & \text{if } 0<t<3 \\ 0 & \text{if } 3<t<7 \\ -\frac{25}{4} & \text{if } 7<t<11 \\ -\frac{5}{2} & \text{if } 11<t<15 \end{cases}$

$a(t)$ does not exist at $t=3$, $t=7$, and $t=11$.

112. Since f' is differentiable, it follows that f' is continuous on the interval $[0,3]$. We have $\frac{f'(3)-f'(0)}{3-0}=\frac{-8-(-2)}{3-0}=\frac{-6}{3}=-2$.

By the Mean Value Theorem, there is at least one real number c with $0<c<3$ such that $f''(c)=-2$.

LEVEL 4: INTEGRATION

113. D
114. D
115. C
116. A
117. E
118. B
119. D
120. $\frac{1}{4}\int_0^4 G(t)dt \approx \frac{1}{4}[2G(1) + 2G(3)] = \mathbf{4.5}$ **pints**.

$\frac{1}{4}\int_0^4 G(t)dt$ is the average amount of gasoline in the bucket, in pints, over the time interval $0 \le t \le 4$ minutes.

121. $y = 1 - \ln\left(-\frac{x^4}{2} + 5x - \frac{7}{2}\right)$
122. -3
123. $\int_0^{15} v(t)\, dt = \mathbf{302.5}$.

The bus travels 302.5 feet in these 15 seconds.

124. $-\frac{4}{3}$
125. 84.577, $5000 - \int_0^T R(t)\, dt = 1000$
126. $\int_0^{15}|v(t)|\, dt$ is the total distance, in miles, that Joe drove during the 15 minutes from $t = 0$ to $t = 15$. $\int_0^{15}|v(t)|\, dt = 4$ miles

127. $\int_1^{11} f(x)\, dx \approx 3 \cdot 4 + 5 \cdot 1 + 1 \cdot 2 + (-3) \cdot 3 = 10$

128. 284.202

LEVEL 5: FREE RESPONSE QUESTIONS

129.

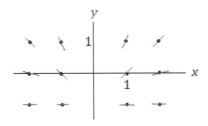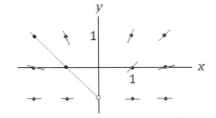

$\frac{dy}{dx} = -1 \Longleftrightarrow y = -x - 1$

130. $y = -\frac{1}{2}x - 1$, $f(-1.5) \approx -\frac{1}{4}$ or $-.25$

131. $f(x) = -\frac{1}{2}x - 1$

132. The region is empty

133. The average rate of change of $S(t)$ over $0 \le t \le 20$ is $\frac{S(20)-S(0)}{20-0} = 175.230$ (or 175.231).

So the average rate of change in the annual salary of an NBA player from 1980 through 2000 was \$175,230 (or \$175,231) per year

134. $S'(10) = 120.112$

The average annual salary of an NBA player is increasing at a rate of \$120,112 per year at the beginning of 1990.

135. $\frac{1}{20} \approx 1508.911$ or 1508.912

This approximation is an overestimate, because a right Riemann sum is used and the function S is strictly increasing.

136. 1992

137. $F(8) = 2\pi + 2$

$F(-1) = \frac{7}{2}$

138. $F'(-4) = f(-4) = 2$

$F''(-4) = f'(-4) = -1$

$F'(6) = f(6) = 0$

$F''(6) = f'(6)$ which does not exist because the graph of f has a "cusp" at $x = 6$.

139. The graph of F is increasing when $F' = f > 0$ (or equivalently, the graph of f is above the x-axis). The graph of F is concave up when $F'' = f' > 0$, or equivalently when f is increasing. f is above the x-axis and increasing on the intervals $2 < x < 4$ and $6 < x < 8$.

140. $F'(x) = f(x) = 0$ when $x = -2$, $x = 2$, and $x = 6$.

$F' = f$ changes sign from positive to negative at $x = -2$. Therefore F has a **relative maximum** at $x = -2$.

$F' = f$ changes sign from negative to positive at $x = 2$. Therefore F has a **relative minimum** at $x = 2$.

$F' = f$ does not change sign at $x = 6$. Therefore F has **neither** a relative minimum nor a relative maximum at $x = 6$.

141. The graph of F has a point of inflection at $x = 0$, $x = 4$, and $x = 6$ because $F'' = f'$ changes sign at each of these values.

142. We will evaluate F at each critical number of F and the two endpoints of the interval.

$F(-5) = -\frac{1}{2}, F(-2) = 4, F(2) = 0,$

$F(6) = 2\pi, F(8) = 2\pi + 2$

The absolute min of F on $[-5,8]$ is $F(-5) = -\frac{1}{2}$.

The absolute max of F on $[-5,8]$ is $F(8) = 2\pi + 2$.

143. $\frac{5}{4}$ or 1.25

144. $y + 1 = 3(x - 1)$

145. $y - 6.797 = 1.563(x + 0.5)$

146. 93.216

147. 3.420

148. $\int_{.934}^{a}(-x^6 + 3.5x^4 - 2)\, dx = \int_{a}^{1.822}(-x^6 + 3.5x^4 - 2)\, dx$

149. Since h and k are twice-differentiable, they are continuous. It follows that f is continuous.

$f(-3) = h\big(k(-3)\big) = h(1) = -4, f(2) = h\big(k(2)\big) = h(8) = 6.$
Since f is a continuous function satisfying $f(-3) < b < f(2)$, the Intermediate Value Theorem guarantees that there is a value a, with $-3 < a < 2$, such that $f(a) = b$.

150. Since h and k are differentiable, so is f. In particular, f is continuous on $[-3,2]$ and differentiable on $(-3,2)$. So the Mean Value Theorem guarantees that there is a value c, with

$-3 < c < 2$ such that $f'(c) = \frac{f(2)-f(-3)}{2-(-3)} = 2.$

151. $f'(x) = h'\big(k(x)\big) \cdot k'(x)$

$f'(-3) = h'\big(k(-3)\big) \cdot k'(-3) = h'(1) \cdot k'(-3)$

$f'(2) = h'\big(k(2)\big) \cdot k'(2) = h'(8) \cdot k'(2) .$

Since $h'(1) = k'(2)$ and $h'(8) = k'(-3)$, $f'(-3) = f'(2)$.

Also, since h and k are twice-differentiable, so is f. So f' is differentiable. In particular, f' is continuous on $[-3,2]$ and differentiable on $(-3,2)$. So the Mean Value Theorem guarantees that there is a value d, with $-3 < d < 2$ such that

$f''(d) = \frac{f'(2)-f'(-3)}{2-(-3)} = \frac{0}{2+3} = 0.$

152. f has no points of inflection.

153. $a(4) \approx \mathbf{2.303}$.

The speed of the particle is decreasing at $t = 4$.

154. $t \approx 1.023$ (right), $t \approx 1.447$ (left)

155. 1.493

156. 2.594

157. $v(t) > 0$ for $0 \le t < 1.253$, $v(t) < 0$ for $1.253 < t < 2.171$
$v(t) > 0$ for $2.171 < t < 2.802$, $v(t) < 0$ for $2.802 < t \le 3$
It follows that the particle changes direction at $t = 1.253$, 2.171, and 2.802.

158. $a(t) = 0$ when $t = \mathbf{0}$, $t \approx \mathbf{1.772}$, and $t \approx \mathbf{2.507}$

In interval notation, the particle is speeding up for t in

$(1.253,1.772) \cup (2.171,2.507) \cup (2.802,3]$

159. The particle changes from moving right to moving left at those times t for which $v(t) = 0$ with $v(t)$ changing from positive to negative. This happens at $t = 1.253$, and $t = 2.802$.

The particle's position at $t = 1.253$ is

$$2 + \int_0^{1.253} v(t)\, dt = 2 + \int_0^{1.253} \cos(t^2)\, dt \approx 2.977$$

The particle's position at $t = 2.802$ is

$$2 + \int_0^{2.802} v(t)\, dt = 2 + \int_0^{2.802} \cos(t^2)\, dt \approx 2.803$$

So the particle is farthest to the right at $t = 1.253$

160. -1

LEVEL 1: DIFFERENTIATION

1. $\dfrac{d}{dx}\left[\dfrac{x \ln e^{x^5}}{6}\right] =$

    (A) $6x^5$

    (B) x^5

    (C) $6x^5 + x^6$

    (D) $x^5 + x^6$

    (E) $\dfrac{x^5 + x^6}{6}$

Solution: $\ln e^{x^5} = x^5$, so that $\dfrac{x \ln e^{x^5}}{6} = \dfrac{x \cdot x^5}{6} = \dfrac{1}{6}x^6$. Therefore we have

$\dfrac{d}{dx}\left[\dfrac{x \ln e^{x^5}}{6}\right] = \dfrac{d}{dx}\left[\dfrac{1}{6}x^6\right] = \dfrac{1}{6} \cdot 6x^5 = x^5$, choice (B).

Notes: (1) $f(x) = \log_e x$ is called the *natural logarithmic function* and is usually abbreviated as $f(x) = \ln x$.

(2) Here are two ways to simplify $\ln e^{x^5}$.

<u>Method 1</u>: Recall that $\ln e = 1$. We have $\ln e^{x^5} = x^5 \ln e = x^5(1) = x^5$. Here we have used the last law in the following table:

Laws of Logarithms: Here is a review of the basic laws of logarithms.

Law	Example
$\log_b 1 = 0$	$\log_2 1 = 0$
$\log_b b = 1$	$\log_6 6 = 1$
$\log_b x + \log_b y = \log_b(xy)$	$\log_5 7 + \log_5 2 = \log_5 14$
$\log_b x - \log_b y = \log_b\left(\dfrac{x}{y}\right)$	$\log_3 21 - \log_3 7 = \log_3 3 = 1$
$\log_b x^n = n\log_b x$	$\log_8 3^5 = 5\log_8 3$

Method 2: Recall that the functions e^x and $\ln x$ are inverses of each other. This means that $e^{\ln x} = x$ and $\ln e^x = x$. Replacing x by x^5 in the second equation gives $\ln e^{x^5} = x^5$.

(3) Geometrically inverse functions have graphs that are mirror images across the line $y = x$. Here is a picture of the graphs of $y = e^x$ and $y = \ln x$ together with the line $y = x$. Notice how the line $y = x$ acts as a mirror for the two functions.

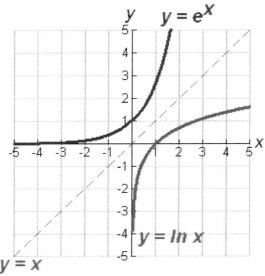

(4) $x \cdot x^5 = x^1 \cdot x^5 = x^{1+5} = x^6$.

Here is a complete review of the laws of exponents:

Law	Example
$x^0 = 1$	$3^0 = 1$
$x^1 = x$	$9^1 = 9$
$x^a x^b = x^{a+b}$	$x^3 x^5 = x^8$
$x^a / x^b = x^{a-b}$	$x^{11}/x^4 = x^7$
$(x^a)^b = x^{ab}$	$(x^5)^3 = x^{15}$
$(xy)^a = x^a y^a$	$(xy)^4 = x^4 y^4$
$(x/y)^a = x^a/y^a$	$(x/y)^6 = x^6/y^6$
$x^{-1} = 1/x$	$3^{-1} = 1/3$
$x^{-a} = 1/x^a$	$9^{-2} = 1/81$
$x^{1/n} = \sqrt[n]{x}$	$x^{1/3} = \sqrt[3]{x}$
$x^{m/n} = \sqrt[n]{x^m} = \left(\sqrt[n]{x}\right)^m$	$x^{9/2} = \sqrt{x^9} = \left(\sqrt{x}\right)^9$

(5) If n is any real number, then the derivative of x^n is nx^{n-1}. This is known as the **power rule**.

Symbolically, $\frac{d}{dx}[x^n] = nx^{n-1}$.

For example, $\frac{d}{dx}[x^6] = 6x^5$.

(6) The derivative of a constant times a function is the constant times the derivative of the function.

Symbolically, $\frac{d}{dx}[cg(x)] = c\frac{d}{dx}[g(x)]$.

For example, $\frac{d}{dx}\left[\frac{1}{6}x^6\right] = \frac{1}{6}\cdot\frac{d}{dx}[x^6] = \frac{1}{6}\cdot 6x^5 = x^5$.

2. If $g(x) = \frac{e^{4x-4}}{4} - \ln(x^2) + (2x-1)^{\frac{5}{2}}$, then $g'(1) =$

   (A) 1
   (B) 2
   (C) 3
   (D) 4
   (E) 5

Solution: $g'(x) = e^{4x-4} - \frac{2}{x} + 5(2x-1)^{\frac{3}{2}}$.

Therefore $g'(1) = 1 - 2 + 5 = 4$, choice (D).

Notes: (1) The derivative of $f(x) = e^x$ is $f'(x) = e^x$.

(2) The derivative of $\ln x$ is $\frac{1}{x}$.

Symbolically, $\frac{d}{dx}[\ln x] = \frac{1}{x}$.

(3) In this problem we need the **chain rule** which says the following:

If $f(x) = (g \circ h)(x) = g(h(x))$, then

$$f'(x) = g'(h(x)) \cdot h'(x)$$

For example, if $f(x) = \ln(x^2)$, then $f(x) = g(h(x))$ where $g(x) = \ln x$ and $h(x) = x^2$. So $f'(x) = g'(h(x)) \cdot h'(x) = \frac{1}{x^2} \cdot 2x = \frac{2}{x}$.

Similarly, we have $\frac{d}{dx}\left[\frac{e^{4x-4}}{4}\right] = \frac{1}{4} \cdot \frac{d}{dx}[e^{4x-4}] = \frac{1}{4}e^{4x-4} \cdot 4 = e^{4x-4}$, and

$$\frac{d}{dx}\left[(2x-1)^{\frac{5}{2}}\right]=\frac{5}{2}(2x-1)^{\frac{3}{2}}(2)=5(2x-1)^{\frac{3}{2}}.$$

(4) If g and h are functions, then $(g+h)'(x)=g'(x)+h'(x)$.

In other words, when differentiating a sum we can simply differentiate term by term.

Similarly, $(g-h)'(x)=g'(x)-h'(x)$.

(5) In the given problem we differentiate each of $\frac{e^{4x-4}}{4}$, $\ln(x^2)$, and $(2x-1)^{\frac{5}{2}}$ separately and then use note (4) to write the final answer.

(6) If we could use a calculator for this problem, we can compute $g'(x)$ at $x=1$ using our TI-84 calculator by first selecting nDeriv((or pressing 8) under the MATH menu, then typing the following:

$$e^{\wedge}(4X-4)/4-\ln(X^{\wedge}2)+(2X-1)^{\wedge}(5/2), X, 1),$$

and pressing ENTER. The display will show approximately 4.

3.   If $x=\ln(t^2+1)$ and $y=\cos 3t$, then $\frac{dy}{dx}=$

   (A) $-\dfrac{3\sin 3t}{t^2+1}$

   (B) $-\dfrac{3\sin 3t}{2t(t^2+1)}$

   (C) $-\dfrac{3(t^2+1)\sin 3t}{2t}$

   (D) $-\dfrac{3\sin 3t}{2t}$

   (E) $2t\sin 3t$

Solution: $\dfrac{dy}{dt}=-3\sin 3t$ and $\dfrac{dx}{dt}=\dfrac{2t}{t^2+1}$. Therefore

$$\frac{dy}{dx}=\frac{\frac{dy}{dt}}{\frac{dx}{dt}}=(-3\sin 3t)\div\frac{2t}{t^2+1}=(-3\sin 3t)\cdot\frac{t^2+1}{2t}=-\frac{3(t^2+1)\sin 3t}{2t}.$$

This is choice (C).

Notes: (1) In this problem we are given a parametrically defined curve. The variable t is called the **parameter**, and the two given equations are called **parametric equations**.

For example, when $t = 0$, we have that $x = \ln(0^2 + 1) = \ln 1 = 0$ and $y = \cos(3 \cdot 0) = 1$. So the point $(0,1)$ is on the given parametrically defined curve, and this point corresponds to the parameter value $t = 0$.

Each value for t corresponds to a point (x, y) in the xy-plane.

(2) The derivative $\frac{dy}{dx}$ is equal to $\frac{\frac{dy}{dt}}{\frac{dx}{dt}}$.

4. If F is the vector-valued function defined by $F(t) = \langle \frac{\ln t}{t}, \cos^2 t \rangle$, then $F''(t) =$

Solution:

$$F'(t) = \langle \frac{t\left(\frac{1}{t}\right) - (\ln t)(1)}{t^2}, 2 (\cos t)(-\sin t) \rangle = \langle \frac{1 - \ln t}{t^2}, -2 \cos t \sin t \rangle, \quad \text{and}$$

$$\text{so } F''(t) = \langle \frac{t^2\left(\frac{-1}{t}\right) - (1 - \ln t)(2t)}{t^4}, -2 \cos t \cos t - 2(\sin t)(-\sin t) \rangle$$

$$= \langle \frac{-t - 2t + 2t \ln t}{t^4}, -2 (\cos^2 t - \sin^2 t) \rangle = \langle \frac{2 \ln t - 3}{t^3}, -2 \cos 2t \rangle.$$

Notes: (1) A 2-dimensional **vector-valued function** F has the form $F(t) = \langle x(t), y(t) \rangle$ where x and y are ordinary functions of the variable t.

A vector-valued function is just a convenient way to give a parametrically defined curve with a single function.

The vector-valued function given in the problem is equivalent to the parametric equations

$$x = \frac{\ln t}{t}, y = \cos^2 t$$

Can you express the parametric equations given in problem 3 as a vector-valued function?

(2) The derivative of the vector-valued function F which is defined by $F(t) = \langle x(t), y(t) \rangle$ is the vector-valued function F' which is defined by $F'(t) = \langle x'(t), y'(t) \rangle$. In other words, we simply differentiate each component.

In this problem we have $x(t) = \frac{\ln t}{t}$ and $y(t) = \cos^2 t$.

Note also that $F''(t) = \langle x''(t), y''(t) \rangle$.

65

(3) To differentiate x we used the **quotient rule** which says the following:

If $f(x) = \frac{N(x)}{D(x)}$, then

$$f'(x) = \frac{D(x)N'(x) - N(x)D'(x)}{[D(x)]^2}$$

I like to use the letters N for "numerator" and D for "denominator."

We needed to use the quotient rule again to differentiate x'.

(4) $\cos^2 t$ is an abbreviation for $(\cos t)^2$. To differentiate y therefore required the chain rule.

(5) To differentiate y' we used the product rule.

LEVEL 1: INTEGRATION

5. If f is a continuous function for all real x, and g is an antiderivative of f, then $\lim_{h \to 0} \frac{1}{h} \int_c^{c+h} f(x)\, dx$ is

   (A) $g(0)$
   (B) $g'(0)$
   (C) $g(c)$
   (D) $g'(c)$
   (E) $g'(f(c)) \cdot f'(c)$

Solution: $\lim_{h \to 0} \frac{1}{h} \int_c^{c+h} f(x)\, dx = \lim_{h \to 0} \frac{1}{h} [g(x)]_c^{c+h}$

$$= \lim_{h \to 0} \frac{g(c+h) - g(c)}{h} = g'(c).$$

This is choice (D).

Notes: (1) The second Fundamental Theorem of Calculus says that if f is a Riemann integrable function on $[a, b]$, then $\int_a^b f(x)\, dx = F(b) - F(a)$ where F is any antiderivative of f.

In this problem, since g is an antiderivative of f, we have $\int_c^{c+h} f(x)\, dx = g(c + h) - g(c)$.

(2) We sometimes use the notation $[F(x)]_a^b$ as an abbreviation for $F(b) - F(a)$.

This is just a convenient way of focusing on finding an antiderivative before worrying about plugging in the **upper** and **lower limits of integration** (these are the numbers b and a, respectively).

In the problem above we have

$$\int_c^{c+h} f(x)\,dx = [g(x)]_c^{c+h} = g(c+h) - g(c)$$

(3) If a function f is continuous on $[a, b]$, then f is Riemann integrable on $[a, b]$.

(4) Recall the definition of the derivative:

$$g'(x) = \lim_{h \to 0} \frac{g(x+h) - g(x)}{h}$$

So we have $g'(c) = \lim_{h \to 0} \frac{g(c+h) - g(c)}{h}$

6. If the function g given by $g(x) = \sqrt{x^3}$ has an average value of 2 on the interval $[0, b]$, then $b = $

(A) $5^{\frac{3}{2}}$

(B) 5

(C) $5^{\frac{2}{3}}$

(D) $5^{\frac{1}{2}}$

(E) $5^{\frac{1}{3}}$

Solution: The average value of g on $[0, b]$ is

$$\frac{1}{b-0} \int_0^b x^{\frac{3}{2}}\,dx = \frac{2}{5b} x^{\frac{5}{2}} \Big|_0^b = \frac{2}{5b} \cdot b^{\frac{5}{2}} = \frac{2}{5} b^{\frac{3}{2}}.$$

So we have $\frac{2}{5} b^{\frac{3}{2}} = 2$. Therefore $b^{\frac{3}{2}} = 5$, and so $b = 5^{\frac{2}{3}}$, choice (C).

Notes: (1) The **average value** of the function f over the interval $[a, b]$ is

$$\frac{1}{b-a} \int_a^b f(x)\,dx.$$

(2) If n is any real number, then an antiderivative of x^n is $\frac{x^{n+1}}{n+1}$.

Symbolically, $\int x^n dx = \frac{x^{n+1}}{n+1} + C$, where C is an arbitrary constant.

For example, $\int x^{\frac{3}{2}} dx = \frac{x^{\frac{5}{2}}}{\frac{5}{2}} + C = x^{\frac{5}{2}} \div \frac{5}{2} + C = x^{\frac{5}{2}} \cdot \frac{2}{5} + C = \frac{2}{5} x^{\frac{5}{2}} + C$.

(3) $\int_a^b f(x)dx = F(b) - F(a)$ where F is any antiderivative of f.

Here, $G(x) = \frac{2}{5} x^{\frac{5}{2}}$ is an antiderivative of the function $g(x) = x^{\frac{3}{2}}$. So $\int_0^b g(x)dx = G(b) - G(0) = \frac{2}{5} b^{\frac{5}{2}} - 0 = \frac{2}{5} b^{\frac{5}{2}}$.

(4) $\frac{1}{b} \cdot b^{\frac{5}{2}} = b^{-1} \cdot b^{\frac{5}{2}} = b^{-1+\frac{5}{2}} = b^{-\frac{2}{2}+\frac{5}{2}} = b^{\frac{3}{2}}$.

It follows that $\frac{2}{5b} \cdot b^{\frac{5}{2}} = \frac{2}{5} \cdot \frac{1}{b} \cdot b^{\frac{5}{2}} = \frac{2}{5} b^{\frac{3}{2}}$.

(5) We solve the equation $\frac{2}{5} b^{\frac{3}{2}} = 2$ by first multiplying each side of the equation by $\frac{5}{2}$. Since $\frac{5}{2} \cdot \frac{2}{5} = 1$, we get $b^{\frac{3}{2}} = 2 \left(\frac{5}{2}\right) = 5$.

We then raise each side of this last equation to the power $\frac{2}{3}$. Since $(b^{\frac{3}{2}})^{\frac{2}{3}} = b^{\frac{3}{2} \cdot \frac{2}{3}} = b^1 = b$, we get $b = 5^{\frac{2}{3}}$.

(6) See problem 1 for a review of the laws of exponents used in notes (4) and (5).

7. $\int_0^\infty 2xe^{-x^2} dx$ is

    (A) -2

    (B) -1

    (C) $\frac{1}{2}$

    (D) 1

    (E) divergent

Solution: $\int_0^\infty 2xe^{-x^2} dx = -e^{-x^2} \big|_0^\infty = 0 - (-1) = 1$, choice (D).

Notes: (1) The given integral is an **improper integral** because one of the limits of integration is ∞. This is actually a **Type II improper integral**. For an example of a Type I improper integral, see problem 21.

(2) $\int_0^\infty f(x)\,dx$ is an abbreviation for $\lim_{b \to \infty} \int_0^b f(x)\,dx$, and $F(x)\,|_0^\infty$ is an abbreviation for $\lim_{b \to \infty} f(x)\,|_0^b$.

In this problem, $f(x) = 2xe^{-x^2}$ and $F(x) = -e^{-x^2}$.

(3) To evaluate the integral $\int 2xe^{-x^2}\,dx$, we can formally make the substitution $u = -x^2$. It then follows that $du = -2x\,dx$.

Uh oh! There is no minus sign inside the integral. But constants never pose a problem. We simply multiply by -1 inside the integral where it is needed, and also outside of the integral sign as follows:

$$\int 2xe^{-x^2}\,dx = -\int -2xe^{-x^2}\,dx$$

We have this flexibility to do this because constants can be pulled outside of the integral sign freely, and $(-1)(-1) = 1$, so that the two integrals are equal in value.

We now have

$$-\int -2xe^{-x^2}\,dx = -\int e^u\,du = -e^u + C = -e^{-x^2} + C.$$

We get the leftmost equality by replacing $-x^2$ by u, and $-2x\,dx$ by du.

We get the second equality by the basic integration formula

$$\int e^u\,du = e^u + C.$$

And we get the rightmost equality by replacing u with $-x^2$.

(4) Note that the function $f(x) = e^{-x^2}$ can be written as the composition $f(x) = g(h(x))$ where $g(x) = e^x$ and $h(x) = -x^2$.

Since $h(x) = -x^2$ is the inner part of the composition, it is natural to try the substitution $u = -x^2$.

Note that the derivative of $-x^2$ is $-2x$, so that $du = -2x\,dx$.

(5) With a little practice, we can evaluate an integral like this very quickly with the following reasoning: The derivative of $-x^2$ is $-2x$. So to integrate $-2xe^{-x^2}$ we simply pretend we are integrating e^x but as we do it we leave the $-x^2$ where it is. This is essentially what was done in the above solution.

69

Note that the $-2x$ "goes away" because it is the derivative of $-x^2$. We need it there for everything to work.

(6) If we are doing the substitution formally, we can save some time by changing the limits of integration. We do this as follows:

$$\int_0^\infty 2xe^{-x^2}\,dx = -\int_0^\infty -2xe^{-x^2}\,dx$$

$$= -\int_0^{-\infty} e^u\,du = -e^u\,\big|_0^{-\infty} = -(0-e^0) = -(-1) = 1.$$

Notice that the limits 0 and ∞ were changed to the limits 0 and $-\infty$, respectively. We made this change using the formula that we chose for the substitution: $u = -x^2$. When $x = 0$, we have that $u = 0$ and when $x = \infty$, we have "$u = -\infty^2 = -\infty \cdot \infty = -\infty$."

I used quotation marks in that last computation because the computation $\infty \cdot \infty$ is not really well-defined. What we really mean is that if we have two expressions that are approaching ∞, then their product is approaching ∞ as well. For all practical purposes, the following computations are valid:

$$\infty \cdot \infty = \infty \qquad \infty + \infty = \infty \qquad -\infty - \infty = -\infty$$

For example, if $\lim_{x\to\infty} f(x) = \infty$ and $\lim_{x\to\infty} g(x) = \infty$, then $\lim_{x\to\infty}[f(x) \cdot g(x)] = \infty$ and $\lim_{x\to\infty}[f(x) + g(x)] = \infty$.

Note that the following forms are **indeterminate**:

$$\frac{\infty}{\infty} \qquad \frac{0}{0} \qquad 0 \cdot \infty \qquad \infty - \infty \qquad 0^0 \qquad 1^\infty \qquad \infty^0$$

For example, if $\lim_{x\to\infty} f(x) = \infty$ and $\lim_{x\to\infty} g(x) = \infty$, then in general we cannot say anything about $\lim_{x\to\infty} \frac{f(x)}{g(x)}$. The value of this limit depends on the specific functions f and g.

8. Let $y = f(x)$ be the solution to the differential equation $\frac{dy}{dx} = \arctan(xy)$ with the initial condition $f(0) = 2$. What is the approximation of $f(1)$ if Euler's method is used, starting at $x = 0$ with a step size of 0.5?

(A) 1

(B) 2

(C) $2 + \frac{\pi}{8}$

(D) $2 + \frac{\pi}{4}$

(E) $2 + \frac{\pi}{2}$

Solution: Let's make a table:

(x, y)	dx	$\dfrac{dy}{dx}$	$dx\left(\dfrac{dy}{dx}\right) = dy$	$(x + dx, y + dy)$
$(0,2)$	$.5$	0	0	$(.5, 2)$
$(.5, 2)$	$.5$	$\dfrac{\pi}{4}$	$\dfrac{\pi}{8}$	$(1, 2 + \dfrac{\pi}{8})$

From the last entry of the table we see that $f(1) \approx 2 + \dfrac{\pi}{8}$, choice (C).

Notes: (1) **Euler's method** is a procedure for approximating the solution of a differential equation.

(2) To use Euler's method we must be given a differential equation $\dfrac{dy}{dx} = f(x, y)$, an initial condition $f(x_0) = y_0$, and a step size dx.

In this problem, we have $\dfrac{dy}{dx} = \arctan(xy)$, $f(0) = 2$, and $dx = 0.5$.

(3) The initial condition $f(x_0) = y_0$ is equivalent to saying that the point (x_0, y_0) is on the solution curve.

So in this problem we are given that $(0,2)$ is on the solution curve.

(4) We can get an approximation to $f(x_0 + dx)$ by using a table (as shown in the above solution) as follows:

In the first column we put the point (x_0, y_0) as given by the initial condition.

In the second column we put the step size dx.

In the third column we plug the point (x_0, y_0) into the differential equation to get $\dfrac{dy}{dx}$.

In the fourth column we multiply the numbers in the previous two columns to get dy.

In the fifth column we add dx to x_0 and dy to y_0 to get the point $(x_0 + dx, y_0 + dy)$. This is equivalent to $f(x_0 + dx) = y_0 + dy$.

(5) We can now copy the point from the fifth column into the first column of the next row, and repeat this procedure to approximate $f(x_0 + 2dx)$.

In this problem, since $x_0 = 0$ and $dx = 0.5$, we have $x_0 + 2dx = 1$, and so we are finished after the second iteration of the procedure.

9. What is the area of the closed region bounded by the curve $y = \ln \sqrt[3]{x}$, and the lines $x = 1$ and $y = -2$?

(A) $\dfrac{e^{-6}+5}{3}$

(B) $\dfrac{e^{-6}+3}{3}$

(C) $\dfrac{e^{-6}+1}{3}$

(D) $\dfrac{e^{-6}-1}{3}$

(E) $\dfrac{e^{-6}-3}{3}$

Solution: First note that $y = \frac{1}{3}\ln x$, so that $3y = \ln x$ and therefore $x = e^{3y}$. So we have

$$\text{Area} = \int_{-2}^{0}(1 - e^{3y})dy = y - \frac{1}{3}e^{3y}\,\Big|_{-2}^{0} = -\frac{1}{3} - \left(-2 - \frac{1}{3}e^{-6}\right) = \frac{e^{-6}+5}{3}.$$

This is choice (A).

Notes: (1) Let's draw a picture of the region.

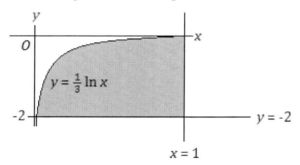

(2) The area between the curves $y = f(x)$ and $y = g(x)$ from $x = a$ to $x = b$ is $\int_a^b |f(x) - g(x)|\,dx$. The x-values a and b are usually the x-coordinates of points of intersection of the two graphs.

In this problem we can let $a = e^{-6}$, $b = 1$, $f x) = \frac{1}{3}\ln x$, $g(x) = -2$. We then have Area $= \int_{e^{-6}}^{1}(\frac{1}{3}\ln x - (-2))dx = \int_{e^{-6}}^{1}(\frac{1}{3}\ln x + 2)dx$. This is a fairly difficult integral that requires integration by parts. We will see how to evaluate this integral in notes (4) and (5) below.

(3) Observe that in the solution above we are thinking of the shaded region as $-2 \le y \le 0$ and $e^{3y} \le x \le 1$ (we already showed that $y = \ln \sqrt[3]{x} = \frac{1}{3}\ln x$ is equivalent to $x = e^{3y}$).

So instead of subtracting the upper curve minus the lower curve inside the integrand, we subtract the rightmost curve minus the leftmost curve. This leads to a much easier integral than the integral we wound up with in note (2). Be aware that a simple substitution is required to integrate e^{3y}, similar to the substitution done in problem 7. I leave the details to the reader.

(4) Note that $\frac{d}{dx}[x \ln x - x] = x\left(\frac{1}{x}\right) + \ln x - 1 = 1 + \ln x - 1 = \ln x$. It follows that $\int \ln x \, dx = x \ln x - x$.

So we can now evaluate the integral given in note (2):

$$\int_{e^{-6}}^{1}\left(\frac{1}{3}\ln x - (-2)\right)dx = \int_{e^{-6}}^{1}\left(\frac{1}{3}\ln x + 2\right)dx$$

$$= \left[\frac{1}{3}(x \ln x - x) + 2x\right]\Big|_{e^{-6}}^{1} = \frac{1}{3}[x \ln x + 5x]\Big|_{e^{-6}}^{1}$$

$$= \frac{1}{3}([0 + 5] - [e^{-6}(-6) + 5e^{-6}]) = \frac{1}{3}(5 + e^{-6}) = \frac{e^{-6}+5}{3}.$$

This is choice (A).

(5) To integrate $\ln x$ formally requires **Integration by Parts**.

Integration by parts is a technique for integrating products of functions. It is quite a bit more complicated than the product rule for derivatives. The integration by parts formula is

$$\int u \, dv = uv - \int v \, du$$

To compute $\int \ln x \, dx$, we can let $u = \ln x$, and $dv = dx$. It then follows that $du = \frac{1}{x}dx$ and $v = x$. So we have

$$\int \ln x \, dx = (\ln x)(x) - \int x\frac{1}{x}dx = x \ln x - \int dx = x \ln x - x + C$$

See problem 23 for more information on integration by parts.

10. Which of the following integrals gives the length of the graph of $y = e^{3x}$ between $x = 1$ and $x = 2$?

(A) $\int_1^2 \sqrt{e^{6x} + e^{3x}}\, dx$

(B) $\int_1^2 \sqrt{x + e^{3x}}\, dx$

(C) $\int_1^2 \sqrt{x + 3e^{3x}}\, dx$

(D) $\int_1^2 \sqrt{1 + 3e^{3x}}\, dx$

(E) $\int_1^2 \sqrt{1 + 9e^{6x}}\, dx$

Solution: $\frac{dy}{dx} = 3e^{3x}$, so that $1 + \left(\frac{dy}{dx}\right)^2 = 1 + 9e^{6x}$. It follows that the desired length is $\int_1^2 \sqrt{1 + 9e^{6x}}\, dx$, choice (E).

Notes: (1) The **arc length** of the differentiable curve with equation $y = f(x)$ from $x = a$ to $x = b$ is

$$\text{Arc length} = \int_a^b \sqrt{1 + \left(\frac{dy}{dx}\right)^2}\, dx$$

(2) By the chain rule, we have $\frac{dy}{dx} = e^{3x}(3) = 3e^{3x}$. See problem 2 for details.

(3) $\left(\frac{dy}{dx}\right)^2 = (3e^{3x})^2 = 3^2(e^{3x})^2 = 9e^{3x \cdot 2} = 9e^{6x}$. See problem 1 for a review of the laws of exponents used here.

LEVEL 1: SERIES

11. The sum of the infinite geometric series $\frac{5}{7} + \frac{15}{28} + \frac{45}{112} + \cdots$ is

Solution: The first term of the geometric series is $a = \frac{5}{7}$, and the common ratio is $r = \frac{15}{28} \div \frac{5}{7} = \frac{15}{28} \cdot \frac{7}{5} = \frac{3}{4}$. It follows that the sum is

$$\frac{a}{1-r} = \frac{\frac{5}{7}}{1 - \frac{3}{4}} = \frac{5}{7} \div \frac{1}{4} = \frac{5}{7} \cdot \frac{4}{1} = \frac{20}{7}.$$

Notes: (1) A **geometric sequence** is a sequence of numbers such that the quotient r between consecutive terms is constant. The number r is called the **common ratio** of the geometric sequence.

For example, consider the sequence

$$\frac{5}{7}, \frac{15}{28}, \frac{45}{112}, \ldots$$

We have $\frac{15}{28} \div \frac{5}{7} = \frac{15}{28} \cdot \frac{7}{5} = \frac{3}{4}$ and $\frac{45}{112} \div \frac{15}{28} = \frac{45}{112} \cdot \frac{28}{15} = \frac{3}{4}$. It follows that the sequence is geometric with common ratio $r = \frac{3}{4}$.

(2) A **geometric series** is the sum of the terms of a geometric sequence. The series in this problem is an **infinite** geometric series.

(3) The sum G of an infinite geometric series with first term a and common ratio r with $-1 < r < 1$ is

$$G = \frac{a}{1 - r}$$

Note that if the common ratio r is greater than 1 or less than -1, then the geometric series has no sum.

(4) As we saw in note (1), we can get the common ratio r of a geometric series, by dividing any term by the term which precedes it.

12. Which of the following series converge?

  I. $\sum_{n=1}^{\infty} \frac{1}{n}$

  II. $\sum_{n=1}^{\infty} \frac{n^3}{2n^3 + 5}$

  III. $\sum_{n=1}^{\infty} \frac{\cos(n\pi)}{n}$

   (A) I only
   (B) II only
   (C) III only
   (D) I and III only
   (E) II, and III only

Solution: The first series is the harmonic series which diverges.

$\lim_{n \to \infty} \frac{n^3}{2n^3 + 5} = \frac{1}{2}$ and so $\sum_{n=1}^{\infty} \frac{n^3}{2n^3 + 5}$ diverges by the divergence test.

$$\sum_{n=1}^{\infty} \frac{\cos(n\pi)}{n} = \sum_{n=1}^{\infty} \frac{(-1)^n}{n}$$

Since $\left(\frac{1}{n}\right)$ is a decreasing sequence with $\lim_{n\to\infty} \frac{1}{n} = 0$, the series $\sum_{n=1}^{\infty} \frac{(-1)^n}{n}$ converges by the alternating series test.

So the answer is choice (C).

Notes: (1) $\sum_{n=1}^{\infty} \frac{1}{n} = 1 + \frac{1}{2} + \frac{1}{3} + \frac{1}{4} + \cdots$ is called the **harmonic series**. This series **diverges**.

It is not at all obvious that this series diverges, and one of the reasons that it is not obvious is because it diverges so slowly.

The advanced student might want to show that given any $M > 0$, there is a positive integer k such that $1 + \frac{1}{2} + \frac{1}{3} + \cdots + \frac{1}{k} > M$. This would give a proof that the harmonic series diverges.

(2) The **divergence test** or **nth term test** says:

(i) if $\sum_{n=1}^{\infty} a_n$ converges, then $\lim_{n\to\infty} a_n = 0$, or equivalently

(ii) if $\lim_{n\to\infty} a_n \neq 0$, then $\sum_{n=1}^{\infty} a_n$ diverges.

Note that statements (i) and (ii) are **contrapositives** of each other, and are therefore **logically equivalent**.

It is usually easier to apply the divergence test by using statement (ii).

In other words, simply check the limit of the underlying *sequence* of the series. If this limit is not zero, then the *series* diverges.

In this problem, the limit of the underlying sequence is $\frac{1}{2}$. Since this is not zero, the given series diverges.

(3) The **converse** of the divergence test is *false*. In other words, if $\lim_{n\to\infty} a_n = 0$, it does not necessarily follow that $\sum_{n=1}^{\infty} a_n$ converges.

Students make this mistake all the time! It is absolutely necessary for $\lim_{n\to\infty} a_n = 0$ for the series to have any chance of converging. But it is not enough! A simple counterexample is the harmonic series.

To summarize: (a) if $\lim_{n\to\infty} a_n \neq 0$, then $\sum_{n=1}^{\infty} a_n$ diverges.

(b) if $\lim_{n\to\infty} a_n = 0$, then $\sum_{n=1}^{\infty} a_n$ may converge or diverge.

(4) To see that $\cos(n\pi) = (-1)^n$, first note that $\cos(0\pi) = \cos 0 = 1$. It follows that $\cos(2k\pi) = \cos(0 + 2k\pi) = 1$ for all integers n, or equivalently, $\cos(n\pi) = 1$ whenever n is even.

Next note that $\cos(1\pi) = \cos\pi = -1$. It then follows that $\cos((2k+1)\pi) = \cos(\pi + 2k\pi) = \cos\pi = -1$ for all integers n, or equivalently, $\cos(n\pi) = -1$ whenever n is odd.

Finally note that $(-1)^n = \begin{cases} 1 & \text{if } n \text{ is even} \\ -1 & \text{if } n \text{ is odd} \end{cases}$

(5) An **alternating series** has one of the forms $\sum_{n=1}^{\infty}(-1)^n a_n$ or $\sum_{n=1}^{\infty}(-1)^{n+1}a_n$ where $a_n > 0$ for each positive integer n.

For example, the series given in III is an alternating series since it is equal to $\sum_{n=1}^{\infty}\frac{(-1)^n}{n} = \sum_{n=1}^{\infty}(-1)^n(\frac{1}{n})$, and $a_n = \frac{1}{n} > 0$ for all positive integers n.

(6) The **alternating series test** says that if (a_n) is a decreasing sequence with $\lim_{n\to\infty} a_n = 0$, then the alternating series $\sum_{n=1}^{\infty}(-1)^n a_n$ or $\sum_{n=1}^{\infty}(-1)^{n+1}a_n$ converges.

Since for all positive integers n, $n < n + 1$, it follows that $\frac{1}{n} > \frac{1}{n+1}$, and the sequence $\left(\frac{1}{n}\right)$ is decreasing. Also it is clear that $\lim_{n\to\infty}\frac{1}{n} = 0$. It follows that $\sum_{n=1}^{\infty}\frac{(-1)^n}{n}$ converges by the alternating series test.

13. Let f be a decreasing function with $f(x) \geq 0$ for all positive real numbers x. If $\lim_{b\to\infty}\int_1^b f(x)\,dx$ is finite, then which of the following must be true?

   (A) $\sum_{n=1}^{\infty} f(n)$ converges

   (B) $\sum_{n=1}^{\infty} f(n)$ diverges

   (C) $\sum_{n=1}^{\infty}\frac{1}{f(n)}$ converges

   (D) $\sum_{n=1}^{\infty}\frac{1}{f(n)}$ diverges

   (E) $\sum_{n=1}^{\infty}[f(n) + \frac{1}{f(n)}]$ converges

Solution: By the integral test, $\sum_{n=1}^{\infty} f(n)$ converges, choice (A).

Notes: (1) The **integral test** says the following:

Let f be a continuous, positive, decreasing function on $[c, \infty)$. Then $\sum_{n=c}^{\infty} f(n)$ converges if and only if $\int_c^{\infty} f(x)\, dx$ converges.

(2) $\int_1^{\infty} f(x)\, dx = \lim_{b \to \infty} \int_1^b f(x)\, dx.$

(3) The integral test cannot be used to evaluate $\sum_{n=1}^{\infty} f(n)$. In general $\sum_{n=1}^{\infty} f(n) \neq \int_1^{\infty} f(x)\, dx.$

(4) The condition of f decreasing can actually be weakened to f "eventually decreasing." For example, $f(x) = \frac{\ln x}{x}$ is not decreasing on $[1, \infty)$, but is decreasing eventually. This can be verified by using the first derivative test (I leave the details to the reader since this is a Calculus AB problem – see problem 48 above in the last section on Calculus AB problems for details on how to apply this test).

Now, $\int_1^{\infty} \frac{\ln x}{x} dx = \frac{1}{2}(\ln x)^2 \Big|_1^{\infty} = \lim_{b \to \infty}(\ln b)^2 = \infty$. It follows that $\int_1^{\infty} \frac{\ln x}{x} dx$ diverges. By the integral test $\sum_{n=1}^{\infty} \frac{\ln n}{n}$ diverges.

(5) For details on how to integrate $\int \frac{\ln x}{x} dx$, see the solution to problem 53 above in the last section on Calculus AB problems.

14. Which of the following series converge to -1 ?

$\quad$ I. $\sum_{n=1}^{\infty} \frac{3}{(-2)^n}$

$\quad$ II. $\sum_{n=1}^{\infty} \frac{1-3n^2}{3n^2+2}$

$\quad$ III. $\sum_{n=1}^{\infty} \frac{1}{n(n+1)}$

$\quad$ (A) I only
$\quad$ (B) II only
$\quad$ (C) III only
$\quad$ (D) I and III only
$\quad$ (E) II, and III only

Solution: The first series is geometric with first term $a = -\frac{3}{2}$ and common ratio $r = -\frac{1}{2}$. So the sum is $\sum_{n=1}^{\infty} \frac{3}{(-2)^n} = \frac{-\frac{3}{2}}{1+\frac{1}{2}} = -1$.

$\lim_{n \to \infty} \frac{1-3n^2}{3n^2+2} = -1$ and so $\sum_{n=1}^{\infty} \frac{1-3n^2}{3n^2+2}$ diverges by the divergence test.

78

$$\sum_{n=1}^{\infty} \frac{1}{n(n+1)} = \sum_{n=1}^{\infty} \left(\frac{1}{n} - \frac{1}{n+1}\right)$$

$$= \lim_{n\to\infty}\left[\left(1 - \frac{1}{2}\right) + \left(\frac{1}{2} - \frac{1}{3}\right) + \cdots + \left(\frac{1}{n} - \frac{1}{n+1}\right)\right] = \lim_{n\to\infty}\left(1 - \frac{1}{n+1}\right) = 1.$$

So the answer is choice (A).

Notes: (1) See problem 11 for more information on infinite geometric series.

(2) For the first series it might help to write out the first few terms:

$$\sum_{n=1}^{\infty} \frac{3}{(-2)^n} = -\frac{3}{2} + \frac{3}{4} - \frac{3}{8} + \cdots + \frac{3}{(-2)^n} + \cdots$$

It is now easy to check that the series is geometric by checking the first two quotients: $\frac{3}{4} \div \left(-\frac{3}{2}\right) = \frac{3}{4} \cdot \left(-\frac{2}{3}\right) = -\frac{1}{2}$, $-\frac{3}{8} \div \frac{3}{4} = -\frac{3}{8} \cdot \frac{4}{3} = -\frac{1}{2}$.

So we see that the series is geometric with common ratio $r = -\frac{1}{2}$. It is also quite clear that the first term is $a = -\frac{3}{2}$.

(3) A geometric series has the form $\sum_{n=0}^{\infty} ar^n$. In this form, the first term is a and the common ratio is r. I wouldn't get too hung up on this form though. Once you recognize that a series is geometric, it's easy enough to just write out the first few terms and find the first term and common ratio as we did in note (2) above.

If we were to put the given series in this precise form it would look like this: $\sum_{n=0}^{\infty} \left(-\frac{3}{2}\right)\left(-\frac{1}{2}\right)^n$. But again, this is unnecessary (and confusing).

(4) See problem 12 for more information on the divergence test.

(5) The third series is a **telescoping sum**. We can formally do a partial fraction decomposition to see that $\sum_{n=1}^{\infty} \frac{1}{n(n+1)} = \sum_{n=1}^{\infty} \left(\frac{1}{n} - \frac{1}{n+1}\right)$. We start by writing $\frac{1}{n(n+1)} = \frac{A}{n} + \frac{B}{n+1}$. Now multiply each side of this equation by $n(n+1)$ to get $1 = A(n+1) + Bn = An + A + Bn$.

So we have $0n + 1 = (A+B)n + A$. Equating coefficients gives us $A + B = 0$ and $A = 1$, from which we also get $B = -1$.

So $\frac{1}{n(n+1)} = \frac{A}{n} + \frac{B}{n+1} = \frac{1}{n} + \frac{(-1)}{n+1} = \frac{1}{n} - \frac{1}{n+1}$.

(6) Another way to find A and B in the equation $1 = A(n + 1) + Bn$ is to substitute in specific values for n. Two good choices are $n = 0$ and $n = -1$.

$n = 0$: $1 = A(0 + 1) + B(0) = A$. So $A = 1$.

$n = -1$: $1 = A(-1 + 1) + B(-1)$. So $1 = -B$, and $B = -1$.

    15. Which of the following series diverge?

        I. $\sum_{n=1}^{\infty} \dfrac{e^n}{n^2+1}$

        II. $\sum_{n=1}^{\infty} (\dfrac{99}{100})^n$

        III. $\sum_{n=1}^{\infty} \dfrac{2^n}{n!}$

        (A) I only
        (B) II only
        (C) III only
        (D) I and III only
        (E) II, and III only

Solution: $\lim_{n \to \infty} \dfrac{e^n}{n^2+1} = \infty$ and so $\sum_{n=1}^{\infty} \dfrac{e^n}{n^2+1}$ diverges by the divergence test.

$\sum_{n=1}^{\infty}(\dfrac{99}{100})^n$ is geometric with common ratio $r = \dfrac{99}{100} < 1$, and so $\sum_{n=1}^{\infty}(\dfrac{99}{100})^n$ converges.

$\lim_{n \to \infty} \left| \dfrac{\frac{2^{n+1}}{(n+1)!}}{\frac{2^n}{n!}} \right| = \lim_{n \to \infty} \left| \dfrac{2^{n+1}}{(n+1)!} \cdot \dfrac{n!}{2^n} \right| = \lim_{n \to \infty} \dfrac{2}{n+1} = 0 < 1,$ and so $\sum_{n=1}^{\infty} \dfrac{2^n}{n!}$ converges by the ratio test.

Therefore the answer is choice (A).

Notes: (1) See problems 11 and 14 for more information on infinite geometric series, and see problem 12 for more information on the divergence test.

(2) We say that the series $\sum_{n=0}^{\infty} a_n$ **converges absolutely** if $\sum_{n=0}^{\infty}|a_n|$ converges. If a series converges absolutely, then it converges.

A series which is convergent, but not absolutely convergent is said to **converge conditionally**.

(3) The Ratio Test: For the series $\sum_{n=0}^{\infty} a_n$, define $L = \lim_{n \to \infty} \left| \frac{a_{n+1}}{a_n} \right|$.

If $L < 1$, then the series converges absolutely, and therefore converges. If $L > 1$, then the series diverges. If $L = 1$, then the ratio test fails.

For the series $\sum_{n=1}^{\infty} \frac{2^n}{n!}$ given in this problem, we have $a_n = \frac{2^n}{n!}$, and so $a_{n+1} = \frac{2^{n+1}}{(n+1)!}$.

16. What are all values of x for which the series $\sum_{n=1}^{\infty} \frac{5^n x^n}{n}$ converges?

   (A) All x except $x = 0$
   (B) $|x| < \frac{1}{5}$
   (C) $|x| > \frac{1}{5}$
   (D) $-\frac{1}{5} < x < \frac{1}{5}$
   (E) $-\frac{1}{5} \le x < \frac{1}{5}$

Solution: $\lim_{n \to \infty} \left| \frac{\frac{5^{n+1} x^{n+1}}{(n+1)}}{\frac{5^n x^n}{n}} \right| = \lim_{n \to \infty} \left| \frac{5^{n+1} x^{n+1}}{n+1} \cdot \frac{n}{5^n x^n} \right| = 5|x|$. So by the ratio test, the series converges for all x such that $5|x| < 1$, or equivalently $|x| < \frac{1}{5}$. Removing the absolute values gives $-\frac{1}{5} < x < \frac{1}{5}$.

We still need to check the endpoints. When $x = \frac{1}{5}$, we get the divergent harmonic series $\sum_{n=1}^{\infty} \frac{1}{n}$, and when $x = -\frac{1}{5}$ we get the convergent alternating series $\sum_{n=1}^{\infty} (-1)^n \frac{1}{n}$. So the series diverges at $x = \frac{1}{5}$ and converges at $x = -\frac{1}{5}$.

The answer is therefore choice (E).

Notes: (1) A **power series** about $x = 0$ is a series of the form $\sum_{n=1}^{\infty} a_n x^n$. To determine where a power series converges we use the ratio test. In other words we compute

$$L = \lim_{n \to \infty} \left| \frac{a_{n+1} x^{n+1}}{a_n x^n} \right| = \lim_{n \to \infty} \left| \frac{a_{n+1}}{a_n} \right| |x|.$$

If $L = 0$, then the series converges only for $x = 0$.

If $L = \infty$, then the series converges absolutely for all x (and therefore converges for all x – see problem 15, note 2).

Otherwise we solve the equation $L < 1$ for $|x|$ to get an inequality of the form $|x| < R$. In this case the series converges absolutely for $|x| < R$ and diverges for $|x| > R$. The positive number R is called the **radius of convergence** of the power series.

As always the ratio test fails when $L = 1$. So the endpoints $x = -R$ and $x = R$ have to be checked separately.

(2) In this problem we have

$$L = \lim_{n \to \infty} \left| \frac{\frac{5^{n+1}x^{n+1}}{(n+1)}}{\frac{5^n x^n}{n}} \right| = \lim_{n \to \infty} \left| \frac{5^{n+1}x^{n+1}}{n+1} \cdot \frac{n}{5^n x^n} \right| = \lim_{n \to \infty} \frac{n}{n+1} \cdot 5|x| = 5|x|$$

Setting $L < 1$ gives $5|x| < 1$, or equivalently $|x| < \frac{1}{5}$. So the radius of convergence is $R = \frac{1}{5}$.

Note that we needed to check the endpoints $x = -\frac{1}{5}$ and $x = \frac{1}{5}$ separately.

LEVEL 2: DIFFERENTIATION

17. Write an equation of the normal line to the curve $y = \sqrt{25 - x}$ at the point $(0,5)$.

Solution: $y' = -\frac{1}{2\sqrt{25-x}}$, so that the slope of the tangent line to y at $(0,5)$ is $y'\big|_{x=0} = -\frac{1}{2\sqrt{25}} = -\frac{1}{2 \cdot 5} = -\frac{1}{10}$. So the slope of the normal line is 10.

An equation of the normal line is then $y = 10x + 5$.

Notes: (1) To find the slope of the tangent line to a curve y at $x = x_0$ we take the derivative y', and substitute in x_0 for x.

In this problem, we used the chain rule to find y', and then substituted 0 in for x. See problem 2 for more information on the chain rule.

(2) The **normal line** to a curve is perpendicular to the tangent line. Therefore the slope of the normal line is the negative reciprocal of the slope of the tangent line.

(3) We wrote an equation of the line in **slope-intercept** form. We have $y = mx + b$, where m is the slope of the line and the point $(0, b)$ is the y-intercept of the line.

18. A curve is described by the parametric equations $x = 3t^2 - 4t$ and $y = \sqrt{4t + 1}$. An equation of the line tangent to the curve at the point where $t = 2$ is

(A) $3x - y = 0$
(B) $12y - x = 32$
(C) $12x - y = 32$
(D) $x - 12y = 32$
(E) $y - 12x = 32$

Solution: When $t = 2$, $x = 3(2)^2 - 4 \cdot 2 = 4$ and $y = \sqrt{4(2) + 1} = 3$. So the point $(4, 3)$ is on the tangent line.

$\dfrac{dy}{dt} = \dfrac{2}{\sqrt{4t+1}}$ and $\dfrac{dx}{dt} = 6t - 4$, and so $\dfrac{dy}{dt}\Big|_{t=2} = \dfrac{2}{\sqrt{4(2)+1}} = \dfrac{2}{3}$ and $\dfrac{dx}{dt}\Big|_{t=2} = 6(2) - 4 = 8$.

It follows that the slope of the tangent line when $t = 2$ is

$$m = \frac{dy}{dx}\Big|_{t=2} = \frac{\frac{dy}{dt}\big|_{t=2}}{\frac{dx}{dt}\big|_{t=2}} = \frac{2}{3} \div 8 = \frac{2}{3} \cdot \frac{1}{8} = \frac{1}{12}.$$

So an equation of the tangent line in point–slope form is

$$y - 3 = \frac{1}{12}(x - 4).$$

Multiplying each side of this equation by 12 yields $12y - 36 = x - 4$. So we get the equation $12y - x = 32$, choice (B).

Notes: (1) See problem 3 for more information on parametric equations.

(2) As usual, the slope of the tangent line to the curve is $\dfrac{dy}{dx}$. In this case we have $\dfrac{dy}{dx} = \dfrac{\frac{dy}{dt}}{\frac{dx}{dt}}$.

(3) The **point-slope form of an equation of a line** is

$$y - y_0 = m(x - x_0)$$

where m is the slope of the line and (x_0, y_0) is any point on the line.

It is generally easiest to write an equation of a line in point-slope form once the slope of the line and a point on the line are known. In this problem, the slope is $\frac{1}{12}$ and the point is $(4,3)$.

19. The line perpendicular to the tangent line to the curve represented by the equation $y = x^2 + 3x + 2$ at the point $(-3,2)$ also intersects the curve at $x =$

    (A) $\frac{1}{3}$

    (B) 2

    (C) 3

    (D) $\frac{7}{2}$

    (E) 6

Solution: $y' = 2x + 3$, so that $y'|_{x=-3} = 2(-3) + 3 = -6 + 3 = -3$. So the slope of the line perpendicular to the tangent line is $m = \frac{1}{3}$. An equation of this line is $y - 2 = \frac{1}{3}(x + 3)$, or equivalently $y = \frac{1}{3}x + 3$.

We now solve the equation $\frac{1}{3}x + 3 = x^2 + 3x + 2$ for x to get

$$x + 9 = 3x^2 + 9x + 6$$
$$0 = 3x^2 + 8x - 3$$
$$0 = (3x - 1)(x + 3)$$

So $3x - 1 = 0$, and therefore $x = \frac{1}{3}$, choice (A).

20. If $\frac{d}{dx}[k(x)] = h(x)$ and if $g(x) = 2x^3 - 5$, then $\frac{d}{dx}[k(g(x))] =$

    (A) $(2x^3 - 5)h(2x^3 - 5)$
    (B) $6x^2h(2x^3 - 5)$
    (C) $h'(x)$
    (D) $6x^2h(x)$
    (E) $h(2x^3 - 5)$

Solution: $\frac{d}{dx}[k(g(x))] = k'(g(x)) \cdot g'(x) = h(2x^3 - 5) \cdot 6x^2$. So the answer is choice (B).

Note: We used the chain rule here. See problem 2 for more information.

21. $\int_1^3 \frac{dx}{(2-x)^3} dx$ is

    (A) -1

    (B) $\ \ 0$

    (C) $\ \ \frac{1}{2}$

    (D) $\ \ 1$

    (E) divergent

Solution: $\int_1^3 \frac{dx}{(2-x)^3} dx = \int_1^2 \frac{dx}{(2-x)^3} dx + \int_2^3 \frac{dx}{(2-x)^3} dx.$

Now, $\int_1^2 \frac{dx}{(2-x)^3} = \lim_{t \to 2^-} \frac{1}{2(2-x)^2} \Big|_1^t.$

Since $\lim_{t \to 2^-} \frac{1}{2(2-t)^2} = +\infty$, it follows that the improper integral is divergent, choice (E).

Notes: (1) The given integral is an **improper integral** because the function $\frac{1}{(2-x)^3}$ has a discontinuity at $x = 2$, and 2 is in the interval $[1,3]$. In other words the integrand has a discontinuity inside the interval of integration. This is a **Type I improper integral**. For an example of a Type II improper integral, see problem 7.

(2) If f has a discontinuity at $x = a$, then

$$\int_a^b f(x)\,dx = \lim_{t \to a^+} \int_t^b f(x)\,dx$$

If f has a discontinuity at $x = b$, then

$$\int_a^b f(x)\,dx = \lim_{t \to b^-} \int_a^t f(x)\,dx$$

If f has a discontinuity at $x = c$, and $a < c < b$, then

$$\int_a^b f(x)\,dx = \int_a^c f(x)\,dx + \int_c^b f(x)\,dx$$

In this last case, $\int_a^b f(x)\,dx$ only converges if both $\int_a^c f(x)\,dx$ and $\int_c^b f(x)\,dx$ converge.

(3) To evaluate the integral $\int \frac{dx}{(2-x)^3}$, we can formally make the substitution $u = 2 - x$. It then follows that $du = -dx$.

So we have $\int \frac{dx}{(2-x)^3} = -\int \frac{-dx}{(2-x)^3} = -\int \frac{du}{u^3} = -\int u^{-3}\,du = -\frac{u^{-2}}{-2} + C$

$$= \frac{1}{2u^2} + C = \frac{1}{2(2-x)^2} + C.$$

(4) By note (2) above we have $\int_1^2 \frac{dx}{(2-x)^3}\,dx = \lim_{t\to 2^-}\int_1^t \frac{dx}{(2-x)^3}$. Then using note (3) we have $\lim_{t\to 2^-}\int_1^t \frac{dx}{(2-x)^3} = \lim_{t\to 2^-} \frac{1}{2(2-x)^2}\big|_1^t$.

$\lim_{t\to 2^-} \frac{1}{2(2-x)^2}\big|_1^t = \lim_{t\to 2^-}\left(\frac{1}{2(2-t)^2} - \frac{1}{2}\right) = \left(\lim_{t\to 2^-} \frac{1}{2(2-t)^2}\right) - \frac{1}{2}.$

For details on how to evaluate $\lim_{t\to 2^-} \frac{1}{2(2-t)^2}$, see the solution to problem 63 above in the last section on Calculus AB problems.

(5) Since $\int_1^2 \frac{dx}{(2-x)^3} = \infty$, we say that $\int_1^2 \frac{dx}{(2-x)^3}$ diverges. By note (2) above it follows that $\int_1^3 \frac{dx}{(2-x)^3}$ diverges.

(6) It is not necessary to compute the second integral, but it can be shown in the same way that $\int_2^3 \frac{dx}{(2-x)^3} = \infty$ as well.

22. Which of the following integrals gives the length of the graph $y = e^{\sqrt{x}}$ between $x = a$ and $= b$?

(A) $\int_a^b \sqrt{\frac{1+e^{2\sqrt{x}}}{4x}}\,dx$

(B) $\int_a^b \sqrt{1 + \frac{1}{4x}e^{2\sqrt{x}}}\,dx$

(C) $\int_a^b \sqrt{e^{\sqrt{x}} + \frac{1}{4x}e^{2\sqrt{x}}}\,dx$

(D) $\int_a^b \sqrt{1 + e^{2\sqrt{x}}}\,dx$

(E) $\int_a^b \sqrt{x + e^{2\sqrt{x}}}\,dx$

Solution: $\frac{dy}{dx} = \frac{1}{2\sqrt{x}}e^{\sqrt{x}}$, and so $\left(\frac{dy}{dx}\right)^2 = \frac{1}{4x}\left(e^{\sqrt{x}}\right)^2 = \frac{1}{4x}e^{2\sqrt{x}}$. So the desired length is $\int_a^b \sqrt{1 + \frac{1}{4x}e^{2\sqrt{x}}}\, dx$, choice (B).

Note: See problem 10 for more information on computing arc length.

23. $\int x \cos 3x\, dx =$

(A) $\frac{x^2}{2}\sin 3x + C$

(B) $\frac{x^2}{6}\sin 3x + C$

(C) $\frac{x}{3}\sin 3x + \frac{1}{3}\cos 3x + C$

(D) $\frac{x}{3}\sin 3x + \frac{1}{9}\cos 3x + C$

(E) $\frac{x}{3}\sin 3x - \frac{1}{9}\cos 3x + C$

Solution: We use integration by parts.

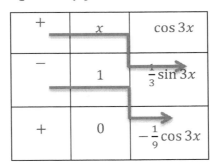

The answer is $\frac{x}{3}\sin 3x + \frac{1}{9}\cos 3x + C$, choice (D).

(1) **Integration by parts** is a technique for integrating products of functions. It is especially useful for integrating products of "different types" of functions. In this problem we are multiplying the polynomial x with the trigonometric function $\cos 3x$. The standard method of integration by parts is by the formula

$$\int u\, dv = uv - \int v\, du$$

To compute $\int x \cos 3x\, dx$, we can let $u = x$, and $dv = \cos 3x\, dx$. It then follows that $du = dx$ and $v = \frac{1}{3}\sin 3x$. So we have

87

$$\int x \cos 3x \, dx = (x)\left(\frac{1}{3}\sin 3x\right) - \int \frac{1}{3}\sin 3x \, dx = \frac{x}{3}\sin 3x + \frac{1}{9}\cos 3x + C$$

(2) In the original solution above, we actually used a shortcut which is sometimes called **tabular integration by parts**.

In the first column we simply alternate signs starting with a plus sign.

In the middle column we put our choice for u, and we differentiate as we go down the column.

In the third column we put our choice for dv, and we integrate as we go down the column.

In this particular example we stop at the third row since we get a 0 in the middle column.

Finally we follow the arrow pattern as seen in the solution above to write down the final answer. As we follow each arrow we multiply, and we add up individual arrows.

(3) How do we figure out how to choose u and dv? There are no absolute rules, but as a general guideline, it is helpful to memorize the mnemonic LIATE.

L stands for Logarithmic, I stands for Inverse Trigonometric, A stands for Algebraic, T stands for Trigonometric, and E stands for exponential.

As a first attempt choose the "leftmost" letter for u and the "rightmost" letter for dv.

In this problem we chose the algebraic function x for u, and the trigonometric function $\cos 3x$ for dv.

(4) For those of you unfamiliar with the term "algebraic function," this class of functions includes polynomials and rational functions, but is more general in the sense that roots can appear in the function as well. For example, $\sqrt{x}$ and $\dfrac{\left(\sqrt[5]{x}+3x^2\right)}{x^{\frac{2}{7}}-5}$ are algebraic, but not polynomial or rational.

(5) The notes at the end of problem 9 show how to integrate $\ln x$ using integration by parts.

(6) The T and E in "LIATE" are generally interchangeable.

24. The area enclosed by the graph of the polar equation $r = 3\sin(2\theta)$ is given by

(A) $9\int_0^{\frac{\pi}{2}}\sin^2(2\theta)\,d\theta$

(B) $18\int_0^{\frac{\pi}{2}}\sin^2(2\theta)\,d\theta$

(C) $18\int_0^{\pi}\sin^2(2\theta)\,d\theta$

(D) $\frac{9}{2}\int_0^{2\pi}\sin^2(2\theta)\,d\theta$

(E) $9\int_0^{2\pi}\sin^2(2\theta)\,d\theta$

Solution: One loop of the graph of $r = 3\sin(2\theta)$ can be graphed from $\theta = 0$ to $\theta = \frac{\pi}{2}$. So the area of one loop of the polar graph is given by

$$A = \frac{1}{2}\int_0^{\frac{\pi}{2}}r^2\,d\theta = \frac{1}{2}\int_0^{\frac{\pi}{2}}[3\sin(2\theta)]^2\,d\theta = \frac{9}{2}\int_0^{\frac{\pi}{2}}\sin^2(2\theta)\,d\theta.$$

The entire graph contains 4 such loops, and so we multiply this area by 4 to get $18\int_0^{\frac{\pi}{2}}\sin^2(2\theta)\,d\theta$, choice (B).

Notes: (1) Let's sketch the graph. The usual "key points" for $r = \sin\theta$ are $\theta = 0, \frac{\pi}{2}, \pi, \frac{3\pi}{2}, 2\pi$. In other words for $r = \sin\theta$ we would substitute multiples of $\frac{\pi}{2}$ in for θ, and connect these points with smooth curves.

But in place of θ we have 2θ. Therefore our first few key points should satisfy $2\theta = 0, \frac{\pi}{2}, \pi, \frac{3\pi}{2}, 2\pi$. Dividing by 2 yields $\theta = 0, \frac{\pi}{4}, \frac{\pi}{2}, \frac{3\pi}{4}, \pi$. In other words for $r = 3\sin 2\theta$ we would substitute multiples of $\frac{\pi}{4}$ in for θ, and connect these points with smooth curves.

So for example, when $\theta = 0$, we have $r = 3\sin 2(0) = 3(0) = 0$. So the point $(0,0)$ is on the graph. As another example, when $\theta = \frac{\pi}{4}$, we have $r = 3\sin 2(\frac{\pi}{4}) = 3\sin\frac{\pi}{2} = 3(1) = 3$. So the point $(\frac{\pi}{4}, 3)$ is on the graph. Note that these are polar points (*not* rectangular). So to plot the point $(\frac{\pi}{4}, 3)$ we form an angle of $\frac{\pi}{4}$ (or 45°) with the positive x-axis, and move outwards 3 units along the terminal ray.

We continue in this fashion as illustrated in the following step-by-step diagram:

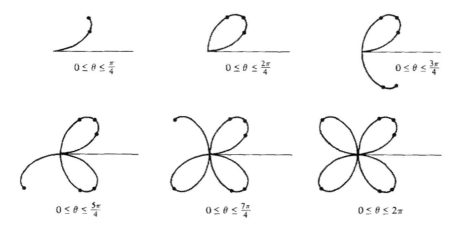

$0 \le \theta \le \frac{\pi}{4}$ $\qquad$ $0 \le \theta \le \frac{2\pi}{4}$ $\qquad$ $0 \le \theta \le \frac{3\pi}{4}$

$0 \le \theta \le \frac{5\pi}{4}$ $\qquad$ $0 \le \theta \le \frac{7\pi}{4}$ $\qquad$ $0 \le \theta \le 2\pi$

(2) From the second picture above we see that one complete loop is graphed from $\theta = 0$ to $\theta = \frac{2\pi}{4} = \frac{\pi}{2}$, and from the last picture we see that there are a total of 4 loops.

(3) The area of the polar curve $r(\theta)$ from $\theta = a$ to $\theta = b$ is $A = \frac{1}{2}\int_a^b r^2\, d\theta$.

In this problem $r = 3\sin(2\theta)$, $a = 0$ and $b = \frac{\pi}{2}$.

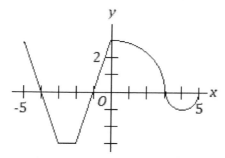

25. Let g be the continuous function defined on $[-5,5]$ whose graph, consisting of three line segments, a quarter circle centered at the origin, and a semicircle centered at $(4,0)$, is shown above. If $G(x) = \int_0^x g(t)\, dt$, where is $G(x)$ nonnegative?

    (A) $[0,5]$ only
    (B) $[-5,-4] \cup [0,5]$ only
    (C) $[-5,-4] \cup [-1,3]$ only
    (D) $[-5,-2] \cup [0,5]$ only
    (E) $[-5,5]$

Solution: If $0 \leq x \leq 5$, then $G(x) = \int_0^x g(t)\, dt$ is positive because the area of the quarter circle is greater than the area of the semicircle.

If $x < 0$, then $G(x) = \int_0^x g(t)\, dt = -\int_x^0 g(t)\, dt$. For this expression to be nonnegative, we need $\int_x^0 g(t)\, dt$ to be nonpositive, and this happens when there is more area below the x-axis than above the x-axis from x to 0. This occurs for $-5 \leq x \leq -2$.

So the answer is choice (D).

Notes: (1) $\int_a^b f(t)\, dt = -\int_b^a f(t)\, dt$.

We used this theorem in the second paragraph to get

$$\int_0^x g(t)\, dt = -\int_x^0 g(t)\, dt.$$

(2) If $a < c < b$, then $\int_a^b f(x)\, dx = \int_a^c f(x)\, dx + \int_c^b f(x)\, dx$.

For example, if $x > 3$, then

$$\int_0^x g(t)\, dt = \int_0^3 g(t)\, dt + \int_3^x g(t)\, dt.$$

(3) Geometrically, if the graph of f lies above the x-axis between a and b, then $\int_a^b f(x)\, dx$ is the area under the graph of f between $x = a$ and $x = b$.

For example, $\int_0^3 g(t)\, dt$ is the area of the quarter circle centered at the origin with radius 3. So $\int_0^3 g(t)\, dt = \frac{\pi}{4}(3^2) = \frac{9\pi}{4}$

If the graph of f lies below the x-axis between a and b, then $\int_a^b f(x)\, dx$ is the negative of the area above the graph of f between a and b.

For example, $\int_3^5 g(t)\, dt$ is the negative of the area of the semicircle centered at $(4,0)$ with radius 1. So $\int_3^5 g(t)\, dt = -\frac{\pi}{2}(1^2) = -\frac{\pi}{2}$.

26. Find the length of the arc of the curve defined by $x(t) = \frac{1}{12}(8t + 16)^{\frac{3}{2}}$ and $y(t) = \frac{t^2}{2}$, from $t = 0$ to $t = 4$.

Solution: $\frac{dx}{dt} = \left(\frac{1}{12}\right)\left(\frac{3}{2}\right)(8t + 16)^{\frac{1}{2}}(8) = \sqrt{8t + 16}$ and $\frac{dy}{dt} = t$. So $\left(\frac{dx}{dt}\right)^2 = 8t + 16$ and $\left(\frac{dy}{dt}\right)^2 = t^2$. So the desired length is

$$\int_0^4 \sqrt{8t + 16 + t^2}\, dt = \int_0^4 \sqrt{t^2 + 8t + 16}\, dt = \int_0^4 \sqrt{(t + 4)^2}\, dt$$

$$= \int_0^4 (t + 4)\, dt = \left(\frac{t^2}{2} + 4t\right)\Big|_0^4 = \frac{4^2}{2} + 4(4) = 8 + 16 = \mathbf{24}.$$

Notes: (1) The **arc length** of the differentiable curve with parametric equations $x = x(t)$ and $y = y(t)$ from $t = a$ to $t = b$ is

$$\text{Arc length} = \int_a^b \sqrt{\left(\frac{dx}{dt}\right)^2 + \left(\frac{dy}{dt}\right)^2}\, dt$$

(2) We used the chain rule to compute $\frac{dx}{dt}$ and a simple power rule to compute $\frac{dy}{dt}$. See problem 2 for more information on the chain rule.

LEVEL 2: SERIES

27. $\sum_{n=2}^{\infty} \frac{1}{n \ln n} =$

   (A) $\frac{1}{\ln(\ln 2)}$

   (B) $\ln(\ln 2)$

   (C) $\frac{1}{\ln 2}$

   (D) $\ln 2$

   (E) The series diverges.

Solution: $\int_2^{\infty} \frac{1}{x \ln x}\, dx = \ln(\ln x)\,\Big|_2^{\infty} = \lim_{b \to \infty} \ln(\ln x)\,\Big|_2^b$

$$= \lim_{b \to \infty} (\ln(\ln b) - \ln(\ln 2)) = \infty.$$

By the integral test $\sum_{n=2}^{\infty} \frac{1}{n \ln n}$ diverges, choice (E).

Notes: (1) Since $f(x) = \frac{1}{x \ln x}$ is a continuous, positive, decreasing function for $x \geq 2$, we can use the integral test to determine if the given sum converges. See problem 13 for more information on the integral test, and see problem 7 for more information on computing the type of improper integral given in this problem.

(2) You should know $\int \frac{1}{x} dx = \ln|x| + C$ (see the solution to problem 22 above in the last section on Calculus AB problems for details.)

(3) To evaluate $\int \frac{1}{x \ln x} dx$, we can formally make the substitution $u = \ln x$. It then follows that $du = \frac{1}{x} dx$. So we have

$$\int \frac{1}{x \ln x} dx = \int \frac{1}{\ln x} \cdot \frac{1}{x} dx = \int \frac{1}{u} du = \ln|u| + C = \ln|\ln x| + C.$$

Since we are considering only $x \geq 2$, it follows that $\ln x > 0$. So we can replace $\ln|\ln x|$ by $\ln(\ln x)$.

(4) With a little practice, we can evaluate an integral like this very quickly with the following reasoning: The derivative of $\ln x$ is $\frac{1}{x}$. So to integrate $\frac{1}{x \ln x}$ we simply pretend we are integrating $\frac{1}{x}$ but as we do it we leave the $\ln x$ where it is. This is essentially what was done in the above solution.

Note that the $\frac{1}{x}$ "goes away" because it is the derivative of $\ln x$. We need it there for everything to work.

28. If $g(x) = \sum_{n=1}^{\infty}(\sin^2 x)^n$, then $g\left(\frac{\pi}{3}\right) =$

(A) $\frac{1}{4}$

(B) $\frac{1}{2}$

(C) $\frac{3}{4}$

(D) 1

(E) 3

Solution: $g\left(\frac{\pi}{3}\right) = \sum_{n=1}^{\infty}\left(\sin^2\left(\frac{\pi}{3}\right)\right)^n = \sum_{n=1}^{\infty}\left(\left(\frac{\sqrt{3}}{2}\right)^2\right)^n = \sum_{n=1}^{\infty}\left(\frac{3}{4}\right)^n$

$$= \frac{\frac{3}{4}}{1-\frac{3}{4}} = \frac{3}{4} \div \frac{1}{4} = \frac{3}{4} \cdot 4 = 3.$$

This is choice (E).

Note: $\sum_{n=1}^{\infty}\left(\frac{3}{4}\right)^n$ is a geometric series with first term $a = \frac{3}{4}$ and common ratio $r = \frac{3}{4}$. See problems 11 and 14 for more information on geometric series.

29. $\sum_{n=1}^{\infty}\left(\frac{3^n}{(7+n^2)^{50}}\right)\left(\frac{(6+n^2)^{50}}{3^{n+1}}\right) =$

    (A) $\frac{1}{7}$

    (B) $\frac{1}{6}$

    (C) $\frac{1}{3}$

    (D) $\frac{3}{7}$

    (E) The series diverges.

Solution: $\lim_{n\to\infty}\left(\frac{3^n}{(7+n^2)^{50}}\right)\left(\frac{(6+n^2)^{50}}{3^{n+1}}\right) = \lim_{n\to\infty}\left(\frac{3^n}{3^{n+1}}\right)\left(\frac{6+n^2}{7+n^2}\right)^{50} = \frac{1}{3}$

By the divergence test, the given series diverges, choice (E).

Notes: (1) See problem 12 for more information on the divergence test.

(2) $\lim_{n\to\infty}\left(\frac{3^n}{3^{n+1}}\right)\left(\frac{6+n^2}{7+n^2}\right)^{50} = \lim_{n\to\infty}\left(\frac{1}{3}\right)\left(\frac{6+n^2}{7+n^2}\right)^{50} = \frac{1}{3}\lim_{n\to\infty}\left(\frac{6+n^2}{7+n^2}\right)^{50}$

$= \frac{1}{3}\left(\lim_{n\to\infty}\frac{6+n^2}{7+n^2}\right)^{50} = \frac{1}{3}(1)^{50} = \frac{1}{3}(1) = \frac{1}{3}.$

(3) Be careful! The sequence $\left(\left(\frac{3^n}{(7+n^2)^{50}}\right)\left(\frac{(6+n^2)^{50}}{3^{n+1}}\right)\right)$ converges to $\frac{1}{3}$. The corresponding series however diverges by the divergence test (because the limit of the sequence is not 0).

30. Find the interval of convergence for the series $\sum_{n=1}^{\infty}\frac{(x-2)^n}{n^3(3^n)}$.

Solution: $\lim_{n\to\infty}\left|\frac{\frac{(x-2)^{n+1}}{(n+1)^3(3^{n+1})}}{\frac{(x-2)^n}{n^3(3^n)}}\right| = \lim_{n\to\infty}\left|\frac{(x-2)^{n+1}}{(n+1)^3(3^{n+1})}\cdot\frac{n^3(3^n)}{(x-2)^n}\right| = \frac{|x-2|}{3}.$ So

by the ratio test, the series converges for all x such that $\frac{|x-2|}{3} < 1$, or equivalently $|x-2| < 3$. Removing the absolute values, we have $-3 < x-2 < 3$, or equivalently $-1 < x < 5$.

We still need to check the endpoints. When $x = 5$, we get the convergent p-series $\sum_{n=1}^{\infty} \frac{1}{n^3}$, and when $x = -1$ we get the absolutely convergent series $\sum_{n=1}^{\infty} (-1)^n \frac{1}{n^3}$. So the series converges for $-1 \le x \le 5$.

Therefore the interval of convergence is $[-1, 5]$.

Notes: (1) See problems 15 and 16 for more information on the ratio test, power series, radius of convergence, and interval of convergence. In problem 16 we looked at a power series about $x = 0$.

(2) A **power series** about $x = a$ is a series of the form $\sum_{n=1}^{\infty} a_n(x - a)^n$. To determine where this power series converges we use the ratio test. In other words we compute

$$L = \lim_{n\to\infty} \left| \frac{a_{n+1}(x-a)^{n+1}}{a_n(x-a)^n} \right| = \lim_{n\to\infty} \left| \frac{a_{n+1}}{a_n} \right| |x - a|.$$

If $L = 0$, then the series converges only for $x = a$.

If $L = \infty$, then the series converges absolutely for all x (and therefore converges for all x – see problem 15, note 2).

Otherwise we solve the equation $L < 1$ for $|x - a|$ to get an inequality of the form $|x - a| < R$. In this case the series converges absolutely for $|x - a| < R$ and diverges for $|x - a| > R$. The positive number R is called the **radius of convergence** of the power series.

As always the ratio test fails when $L = 1$. So the endpoints $x - a = -R$ and $x - a = R$, or equivalently $x = a - R$ and $x = a + R$ have to be checked separately.

(2) In this problem we have

$$L = \lim_{n\to\infty} \left| \frac{\frac{(x-2)^{n+1}}{(n+1)^3(3^{n+1})}}{\frac{(x-2)^n}{n^3(3^n)}} \right| = \lim_{n\to\infty} \left| \frac{(x-2)^{n+1}}{(n+1)^3(3^{n+1})} \cdot \frac{n^3(3^n)}{(x-2)^n} \right|$$

$$= \lim_{n\to\infty} \frac{n^3}{(n+1)^3} \cdot \frac{1}{3} |x - 2| = \frac{1}{3} |x - 2|$$

Setting $L < 1$ gives $\frac{1}{3}|x - 2| < 1$, or equivalently $|x - 2| < 3$. So the radius of convergence is $R = 3$.

(3) We can use the formulas $x = a - R$ and $x = a + R$ to see that the endpoints of the interval are $x = 2 - 3 = -1$ and $x = 2 + 3 = 5$. These need to be checked separately.

Alternatively, we can remove the absolute values and solve for x as was done in the solution above.

(4) A **p-series** is a series of the form $\sum_{n=1}^{\infty} \frac{1}{n^p} = \frac{1}{1^p} + \frac{1}{2^p} + \frac{1}{3^p} + \cdots$

A p-series converges if $p > 1$ and diverges if $p \leq 1$. Note that a 1-series is simply the divergent harmonic series.

In this problem, when $x = 5$ we get a 3-series which converges because $3 > 1$.

When $x = -1$ we get the series $\sum_{n=1}^{\infty} (-1)^n \frac{1}{n^3}$. Since $\left| (-1)^n \frac{1}{n^3} \right| = \frac{1}{n^3}$ and $\sum_{n=1}^{\infty} \frac{1}{n^3}$ converges, the series $\sum_{n=1}^{\infty} (-1)^n \frac{1}{n^3}$ is absolutely convergent, and therefore convergent.

(5) See problem 15 for more information on absolute convergence.

31. The second-degree Taylor polynomial about $x = 0$ of $\ln(2 - 2x)$ is

(A) $-x - \frac{x^2}{2}$
(B) $-x - x^2$
(C) $\ln 2 - x - x^2$
(D) $\ln 2 - x - \frac{x^2}{2}$
(E) $\ln 2 - x + \frac{x^2}{2}$

Solution: Let $f(x) = \ln(2 - 2x)$. Then $f'(x) = -\frac{1}{1-x} = -(1-x)^{-1}$ and $f''(x) = -(1-x)^{-2}$. So we have $f(0) = \ln 2$, $f'(0) = -1$, and $f''(0) = -1$.

The second-degree Taylor polynomial is therefore

$$\ln 2 + (-1)x + \frac{(-1)x^2}{2!} = \ln 2 - x - \frac{x^2}{2}.$$

This is choice (D).

Notes: (1) The nth degree **Taylor polynomial** about $x = 0$ for the function f is

$$P_n(x) = f(0) + f'(0)x + \frac{f''(0)}{2!}x^2 + \frac{f'''(0)}{3!}x^3 + \cdots + \frac{f^n(0)}{n!}x^n$$

For this problem we are being asked for the second degree Taylor polynomial $P_2(x) = f(0) + f'(0)x + \frac{f''(0)}{2!}x^2$.

(2) The following is not needed for this problem but may be useful in similar problems.

More generally, the nth degree **Taylor polynomial** about $x = a$ for the function f is

$$P_n(x) = f(a) + f'(a)(x - a) + \frac{f''(a)}{2!}(x - a)^2 + \frac{f'''(a)}{3!}(x - a)^3 + \cdots + \frac{f^n(a)}{n!}(x - a)^n$$

Using summation notation, we can write

$$P_n(x) = \sum_{k=0}^{n} \frac{f^{(k)}(a)}{k!}(x - a)^k$$

Note that we define $f^{(0)}(a) = f(a)$, and recall that 0! is defined to be 1.

32. If $\sum_{n=0}^{\infty} a_n x^n$ is a Maclaurin series that converges to $g(x)$ for all x. then $g''(1) =$

    (A) 1
    (B) a_2
    (C) $\sum_{n=2}^{\infty} a_n$
    (D) $\sum_{n=2}^{\infty} n(n-1)a_n$
    (E) $\sum_{n=2}^{\infty} n(n-1)a_n^{n-2}$

Solution: $g(x) = \sum_{n=0}^{\infty} a_n x^n$. So we have $g'(x) = \sum_{n=1}^{\infty} na_n x^{n-1}$ and $g''(x) = \sum_{n=2}^{\infty} n(n-1)a_n x^{n-2}$.

So $g''(1) = \sum_{n=2}^{\infty} n(n-1)a_n$, choice (D).

Notes: (1) The **Maclaurin series** for the function f is

$$\sum_{n=0}^{\infty} \frac{f^n(0)}{n!}x^n = f(0) + f'(0)x + \frac{f''(0)}{2!}x^2 + \cdots + \frac{f^n(0)}{n!}x^n + \cdots$$

(2) A Maclaurin series is a special case of a **Taylor series**. More specifically a Maclaurin series is a Taylor series about $x = 0$. See problem 47 for the more general definition.

(3) Taylor series, and more specifically, Maclaurin series can be differentiated term by term. Since the derivative of $a_n x^n$ is $n a_n x^{n-1}$, it follows that the derivative of

$$g(x) = \sum_{n=0}^{\infty} a_n x^n = a_0 + a_1 x + a_2 x^2 + \cdots + a_n x^n + \cdots$$

is

$$g'(x) = \sum_{n=1}^{\infty} n a_n x^{n-1} = a_1 + 2 a_2 x + 3 a_3 x^2 \ldots + n a_n x^{n-1} + \cdots$$

Note that the $n = 0$ term "went away" because the derivative of the constant a_0 is 0.

(4) Differentiating again yields

$$g''(x) = \sum_{n=2}^{\infty} n(n-1) a_n x^{n-1}$$

$$= 2 a_2 + 3 \cdot 2 a_3 x + 4 \cdot 3 a_4 x^2 \ldots + n(n-1) a_n x^{n-2} + \cdots$$

Once again, note that the $n = 1$ term "went away" because the derivative of the constant a_1 is zero.

Substituting 1 in for x yields

$$g''(1) = \sum_{n=2}^{\infty} n(n-1) a_n$$

$$= 2 a_2 + 3 \cdot 2 a_3 + 4 \cdot 3 a_4 \ldots + n(n-1) a_n + \cdots$$

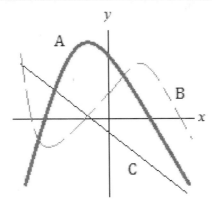

33. Three graphs labeled A, B, and C are shown above. One is the graph of f, one is the graph of f', and one is the graph of f''. Which of the following correctly identifies each of the three graphs in the order f, f', f'' ?

    (A) A, B, C
    (B) A, C, B
    (C) B, A, C
    (D) B, C, A
    (E) C, A, B

Solution: Observe that the x-values where graph B has a relative minimum or maximum are x-intercepts of graph A. Similarly, the x-value where graph A has a relative maximum is an x-intercept of graph C.

So B is the graph of f, A is the graph of f', and C is the graph of f'', choice (C).

Notes: (1) It looks as though B is the graph of a cubic function (3rd degree polynomial), A is the graph of a quadratic function (2nd degree polynomial), and C is the graph of a linear function (1st degree polynomial). Since the derivative of a polynomial is a polynomial of 1 less degree, it follows that B must be the graph of f, A is the graph of f', and C is the graph of f''.

(2) Here are some additional observations we can make to confirm that B is the graph of f, A is the graph of f', and C is the graph of f''.

- When graph B is increasing, graph A is above the x-axis, and when graph B is decreasing, graph A is below the x-axis.

- When graph B is concave up, graph C is above the x-axis, and when graph B is concave down, graph C is below the x-axis.

- When graph A is increasing, graph C is above the x-axis, and when graph A is decreasing, graph C is below the x-axis.

34. A point (x, y) is moving along the curve $y = f(x)$. At the instant when the slope of the curve is $-\frac{2}{5}$, the y-coordinate of the point is decreasing at the rate of 4 units per minute. The rate of change, in units per minute, of the x-coordinate of the point is

   (A) -10

   (B) $-\frac{1}{10}$

   (C) 0

   (D) $\frac{1}{10}$

   (E) 10

Solution: $\frac{dy}{dt} = f'(x) \cdot \frac{dx}{dt}$. So we have $-4 = -\frac{2}{5} \cdot \frac{dx}{dt}$. It follows that $\frac{dx}{dt} = (-4)\left(-\frac{5}{2}\right) = 10$, choice (E).

Notes: (1) Remember that the word *rate* generally indicates a derivative. "Increasing at a rate of" indicates a positive derivative, and "decreasing at a rate of" indicates a negative derivative.

So "the y-coordinate of the point is decreasing at the rate of 4 units per minute" can be interpreted as $\frac{dy}{dt} = -4$.

(2) This is a **related rates** problem. In a related rates problem we differentiate the independent and dependent variables with respect to a new variable, usually named t, for time.

(3) A *related rates* problem can be pictured as a *dynamic* (moving) process that gets fixed at a specific moment in time.

For this problem we can picture a point moving along a curve. We then *freeze time* at the moment when the slope of the curve is $f'(x) = -\frac{2}{5}$.

At this moment in time we want to know what the rate of change of the x-coordinate of the point is. The word "rate" indicates that we want the derivative $\frac{dx}{dt}$.

Don't forget to apply the chain rule when differentiating the right hand side of the equation $y = f(x)$. In this case, the derivative of $f(x)$ is $f'(x) \cdot \frac{dx}{dt}$.

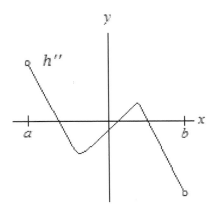

35. Let h be a function whose domain is the open interval (a, b). The figure above shows the graph of h''. Which of the following describes the relative extrema of h' and the points of inflection of the graph of h' ?

    (A) 1 relative maximum, 1 relative minimum, 2 points of inflection

    (B) 1 relative maximum, 2 relative minima, 2 points of inflection

    (C) 1 relative maximum, 2 relative minima, 2 points of inflection

    (D) 2 relative maxima, 1 relative minimum, 2 points of inflection

    (E) 2 relative maxima, 1 relative minimum, 3 points of inflection

Solution: h' has 3 critical numbers. These are the x-values where $h''(x) = 0$. At each of the leftmost and rightmost critical numbers, h' has a relative maximum. At the other critical number, h' has a relative minimum. So h' has 2 relative maxima and 1 relative minimum.

The graph of h' has a point of inflection whenever the graph of h'' has a relative maximum or minimum. This occurs twice, and so the graph of h' has 2 points of inflection.

Therefore the answer is choice (D).

Notes: (1) A **critical number** of a function f is a real number c in the domain of f such that $f'(c) = 0$ or $f'(c)$ is undefined.

(2) A function f attains a **relative minimum** (or **local minimum**) at a real number $x = c$ if there is an interval (a, b) containing c such that $f(c) < f(x)$ for all x in the interval.

If a function is decreasing to the left of c, and increasing to the right of c, then f attains a relative minimum at c.

In terms of derivatives, if $f'(x) < 0$ for $x < c$, and $f'(x) > 0$ for $x > c$, then f attains a relative minimum at c.

A similar analysis can be done for a relative maximum. This method of finding the relative extrema of a function is called the **first derivative test**.

(3) Take careful note that in this problem we are trying to find the relative extrema of the *derivative* of h. So we need to be checking $h''(x)$ near $x = c$.

(4) For the leftmost critical number of h' (in other words the leftmost x-intercept of h''), h'' changes from positive to negative as we go from left to right across the critical number. So h' changes from increasing to decreasing, and the leftmost critical number of h' is a relative maximum.

A similar analysis can be made for the other two critical numbers.

(5) A point at which a function changes concavity is called a **point of inflection**. At a point of inflection, the second derivative of the function is either 0 or undefined.

So we are looking for x-values such that $h'''(x) = 0$. This happens when the graph of h'' has a horizontal tangent line. In the given graph of h'' there are two such places, the relative maximum and minimum values of h''.

36. * Let K be defined by $K(t) = 70 + 15 \cos\left(\frac{\pi t}{4}\right) + 5 \sin(\frac{\pi t}{3})$. For $0 \le t \le 6$, K is decreasing most rapidly when $t =$

Solution: $K'(t) = -\frac{15\pi}{4}\sin\left(\frac{\pi t}{4}\right) + \frac{5\pi}{3}\cos(\frac{\pi t}{3})$. We graph K' in our calculator in the window $[0,6] \times [-20,20]$ and use the "minimum" feature to find that $t \approx 2.431$.

Note: K is decreasing most rapidly when K' is as small as possible.

LEVEL 3: INTEGRATION

37. $\int \frac{1-x}{x^2+3x+2}dx =$

   (A) $\ln|(x+1)(x+2)| + C$
   (B) $\ln|(x+1)^2(x+2)^3| + C$
   (C) $\ln|(x+1)^3(x+2)^2| + C$
   (D) $\ln\left|\frac{(x+2)^3}{(x+1)^2}\right| + C$
   (E) $\ln\left|\frac{(x+1)^2}{(x+2)^3}\right| + C$

Solution: We do a partial fraction decomposition. First note that $x^2 + 3x + 2 = (x+1)(x+2)$, so that $\frac{1-x}{x^2+3x+2} = \frac{1-x}{(x+1)(x+2)}$.

$\frac{1-x}{(x+1)(x+2)} = \frac{A}{x+1} + \frac{B}{x+2}$ if and only if $1 - x = A(x+2) + B(x+1)$.

Letting $x = -1$ yields $A = 2$, and letting $x = -2$ yields $B = -3$. So we have $\frac{1-x}{(x+1)(x+2)} = \frac{2}{x+1} - \frac{3}{x+2}$. It follows that

$$\int \frac{1-x}{x^2+3x+2}dx = \int \frac{2}{x+1} - \frac{3}{x+2}dx = 2\ln|x+1| - 3\ln|x+2|$$

$$= \ln|x+1|^2 - \ln|x+2|^3 = \ln\frac{|x+1|^2}{|x+2|^3} = \ln\left|\frac{(x+1)^2}{(x+2)^3}\right| + C.$$

This is choice (E).

Notes: (1) Note that the rational expression $\frac{1-x}{x^2+3x+2}$ is a **proper fraction** because the degree of the polynomial in the numerator is less than the degree of the polynomial in the denominator.

(2) To integrate a rational function that is expressed as a proper fraction, it often helps to do a **partial fraction decomposition**. This means that we rewrite the fraction as a sum of two or more fractions with denominators of smaller degree.

In this case we attempt to rewrite $\frac{1-x}{(x+1)(x+2)}$ as $\frac{A}{x+1} + \frac{B}{x+2}$. We need to figure out the real numbers A and B.

(3) As seen in the solution above, we begin by multiplying each side of the equation $\frac{1-x}{(x+1)(x+2)} = \frac{2}{x+1} - \frac{3}{x+2}$ by the least common denominator $(x+1)(x+2)$ to get $1 - x = A(x+2) + B(x+1)$.

There are now several ways to find A and B.

Method 1: Substitute $x = -1$ to find A and substitute $x = -2$ to find B.

Method 2: Substitute in *any* two real numbers for x and solve the resulting system of equations. Choosing the values used in Method 1 is most efficient of course.

Method 3: Equate coefficients of corresponding terms. To use this method we multiply out the right hand side, and regroup as follows:

$$-x + 1 = (A + B)x + 2A + B.$$

Now, the coefficient of x on the left is -1 and the coefficient of x on the right is $A + B$. So we have $A + B = -1$.

The constant term on the left is 1 and the constant term on the right is $2A + B$. So we have $2A + B = 1$.

We now solve the resulting system of equations. For example, we can subtract the first equation from the second to get

$$
\begin{aligned}
2A + B &= 1 \\
A + B &= -1 \\
\hline
A \phantom{{}+ B} &= 2
\end{aligned}
$$

Substituting $A = 2$ into $A + B = -1$ gives $2 + B = -1$, or $B = -3$.

(4) See problem 1 for the laws of logarithms that were used here.

38. * Let G be defined by $G(x) = \int_2^x 35e^{-t^2+t+1}(2t^2 - 3t + 5)dt$, Which of the following statements about G must be true?

   I. G is increasing on $(2,3)$.
   II. G is concave up on $(2,3)$
   III. $G(3) > 0$

   (A) I only
   (B) II only
   (C) III only
   (D) I and III only
   (E) II, and III only

Solution: $G'(x) = 35e^{-x^2+x+1}(2x^2 - 3x + 5)$. We graph G' in our calculator in the window $[2,3] \times [0,100]$.

Since the graph of G' lies entirely above the x-axis, $G' > 0$ on $(2,3)$, and therefore G is increasing on $(2,3)$. So I is true.

Since the graph of G' is decreasing, $G'' < 0$ on $(2,3)$, and therefore G is concave down on $(2,3)$. So II is false.

$G(3) = \int_2^3 35e^{-t^2+t+1}(2t^2 - 3t + 5)dt$ is the "net area" between the graph of G' and the x-axis from $x = 2$ to $x = 3$. Since G' lies entirely above the x-axis, $G(3) > 0$. So III is true.

The answer is therefore choice (D).

39. A solid has a rectangular base that lies in the first quadrant and is bounded by the x- and y-axes and the lines $x = 3$ and $y = 1$. The height of the solid above the point (x,y) is $(2 + 5x)^2$. Which of the following is a Riemann sum approximation for the volume of the solid?

   (A) $\sum_{i=1}^{n} \frac{3i}{n}\left(2 + \frac{15i}{n}\right)^2$

   (B) $\sum_{i=1}^{n} \frac{3}{n}\left(2 + \frac{15i}{n}\right)^2$

   (C) $\sum_{i=1}^{n} \frac{3i}{n}\left(2 + \frac{3i}{n}\right)^2$

   (D) $\sum_{i=1}^{n} \frac{3}{n}\left(2 + \frac{3i}{n}\right)^2$

   (E) $\sum_{i=1}^{n} \frac{1}{n}\left(2 + \frac{15i}{n}\right)^2$

Solution: Let $f(x) = (2 + 5x)^2$ and partition the interval $[0,3]$ into n equal subintervals as follows:

Let $x_0 = \frac{3 \cdot 0}{n} = 0$, $x_1 = \frac{3 \cdot 1}{n}$, $x_2 = \frac{3 \cdot 2}{n}$,..., $x_{n-1} = \frac{3(n-1)}{n}$, $x_{100} = \frac{3n}{n} = 3$.

We get the corresponding subintervals $[0, \frac{3}{n}]$, $[\frac{3}{n}, \frac{3 \cdot 2}{n}]$,..., $[\frac{3(n-1)}{n}, 3]$.

The length of each subinterval (and therefore the base of each rectangle) is $\frac{3-0}{n} = \frac{3}{n}$.

For the height of each rectangle we choose the right endpoint of each subinterval x^*, and compute $f(x^*)$.

So the height of the leftmost rectangle will be $f\left(\frac{3}{n}\right) = \left(2 + \frac{15}{n}\right)^2$. It follows that the area of the leftmost rectangle is $\frac{3}{n}\left(2 + \frac{15}{n}\right)^2$.

Similarly, the area of the next rectangle will be $\frac{3}{n}\left(2 + \frac{15 \cdot 2}{n}\right)^2$.

Continuing in this fashion, we get that the area of the rightmost rectangle is $\frac{3}{n}\left(2 + \frac{15 \cdot n}{n}\right)^2$

So we are approximating the volume under the graph of $f(x) = (2 + 5x)^2$ from $x = 0$ to $x = 3$ by

$$\frac{3}{n}\left(2 + \frac{15}{n}\right)^2 + \frac{3}{n}\left(2 + \frac{15 \cdot 2}{n}\right)^2 + \cdots + \frac{3}{n}\left(2 + \frac{15 \cdot n}{n}\right)^2$$

$$= \sum_{i=1}^{n} \frac{3}{n}\left(2 + \frac{15i}{n}\right)^2.$$

This is choice (B).

Notes: (1) For more information on Riemann sums, see problem 119 above in the last section on Calculus AB problems.

(2) The standard geometrical application of Riemann sums is to approximate the area under a curve. This problem is a bit trickier because we are approximating a volume of a solid instead. But in this case, because the height of the rectangle is 1, approximating this volume is exactly the same as approximating the area under the curve $f(x) = (2 + 5x)^2$ from $x = 0$ to $x = 3$.

106

x	$f'(x)$
-2	1
-1	2
0	3
1	4
2	5

40. The table above gives selected values for the derivative of a function f on the interval $-2 \le x \le 2$. If $f(-2) = 3$ and Euler's method with a step size of 2 is used to approximate $f(2)$, what is the resulting approximation?

   (A) 3
   (B) 5
   (C) 7
   (D) 9
   (E) 11

Solution: Let's make a table:

(x, y)	dx	$\frac{dy}{dx}$	$dx\left(\frac{dy}{dx}\right) = dy$	$(x + dx, y + dy)$
$(-2, 3)$	2	1	2	$(0, 5)$
$(0, 5)$	2	3	6	$(2, 11)$

From the last entry of the table we see that $f(2) \approx 11$, choice (E).

Note: See problem 8 for more detailed information on how Euler's method works.

41. Which of the following integrals represents the area enclosed by the smaller loop of the graph of $r = 2 + 4\cos\theta$?

(A) $\int_{\frac{2\pi}{3}}^{\frac{4\pi}{3}} (1 + 2\cos\theta)\, d\theta$

(B) $\int_{\frac{2\pi}{3}}^{\frac{4\pi}{3}} (1 + 2\cos\theta)^2\, d\theta$

(C) $2\int_{\frac{2\pi}{3}}^{\frac{4\pi}{3}} (1 + 2\cos\theta)^2\, d\theta$

(D) $\int_{\frac{4\pi}{3}}^{\frac{7\pi}{3}} (1 + 2\cos\theta)\, d\theta$

(E) $\int_{\frac{4\pi}{3}}^{\frac{7\pi}{3}} (1 + 2\cos\theta)^2\, d\theta$

Solution: The smaller loop of the graph of $r = 2 + 4\cos\theta$ can be graphed from $\theta = \frac{2\pi}{3}$ to $\theta = \frac{4\pi}{3}$. So the area enclosed by this loop is given by

$$A = \frac{1}{2}\int_{\frac{2\pi}{3}}^{\frac{4\pi}{3}} r^2\, d\theta = \frac{1}{2}\int_{\frac{2\pi}{3}}^{\frac{4\pi}{3}} [2 + 4\cos\theta]^2\, d\theta = 2\int_{\frac{2\pi}{3}}^{\frac{4\pi}{3}} [1 + 2\cos\theta]^2\, d\theta.$$

This is choice (C).

Notes: (1) See problem 24 to see how to sketch a polar graph in detail.

(2) The graph of the given polar equation is called a **limacon**. Let's sketch it. We will use the usual key points: $\theta = 0, \frac{\pi}{2}, \pi, \frac{3\pi}{2}, 2\pi$. And we will also find any additional values for θ such that $2 + 4\cos\theta = 0$. Subtracting 2 from each side of this equation gives $4\cos\theta = -2$. So $\cos\theta = -\frac{1}{2}$, and so $\theta = \frac{2\pi}{3}$ and $\theta = \frac{4\pi}{3}$. Let's make a table of values and sketch the graph:

108

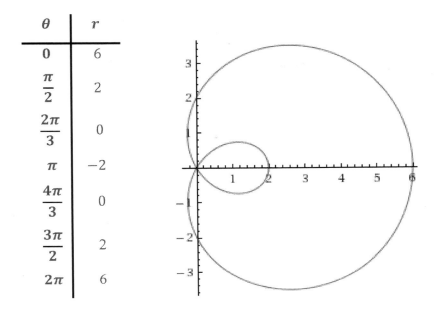

θ	r
0	6
$\dfrac{\pi}{2}$	2
$\dfrac{2\pi}{3}$	0
π	-2
$\dfrac{4\pi}{3}$	0
$\dfrac{3\pi}{2}$	2
2π	6

Note that the smaller loop is traced out from $\theta = \frac{2\pi}{3}$ to $\theta = \frac{4\pi}{3}$. r takes on negative values throughout this whole interval, so there is no danger of positive and negative r-values canceling each other out.

(3) Observe that $\frac{1}{2}\int_{\frac{2\pi}{3}}^{\frac{4\pi}{3}}[2 + 4\cos\theta]^2\, d\theta = \frac{1}{2}\int_{\frac{2\pi}{3}}^{\frac{4\pi}{3}}[2(1 + 2\cos\theta)]^2\, d\theta$

$= \frac{1}{2}\int_{\frac{2\pi}{3}}^{\frac{4\pi}{3}} 4(1 + 2\cos\theta)^2\, d\theta = 2\int_{\frac{2\pi}{3}}^{\frac{4\pi}{3}}[1 + 2\cos\theta]^2\, d\theta$

42. $\int e^{3x}\cos 2x\, dx =$

Solution: We use integration by parts.

$+$	e^{3x}	$\cos 2x$
$-$	$3e^{3x}$	$\frac{1}{2}\sin 2x$
$+$	$9e^{3x}$	$-\frac{1}{4}\cos 2x$

So $\int e^{3x} \cos 2x \, dx = \frac{1}{2} e^{3x} \sin 2x + \frac{3}{4} e^{3x} \cos 2x - \frac{9}{4} \int e^{3x} \cos 2x \, dx.$

We add $\frac{9}{4} \int e^{3x} \cos 2x \, dx$ to each side of this equation to get

$$\frac{13}{4} \int e^{3x} \cos 2x \, dx = \frac{1}{2} e^{3x} \sin 2x + \frac{3}{4} e^{3x} \cos 2x,$$

and so $\int e^{3x} \cos 2x \, dx = \frac{4}{13} \left(\frac{1}{2} e^{3x} \sin 2x + \frac{3}{4} e^{3x} \cos 2x \right) + C.$

Finally, $\int e^{3x} \cos 2x \, dx = \frac{2}{13} e^{3x} \sin 2x + \frac{3}{13} e^{3x} \cos 2x + C.$

Notes: (1) See problem 23 to see how to solve a simple integration by parts problem. This problem is a bit more difficult as it requires two iterations of the integration by parts formula. Recall the formula:

$$\int u \, dv = uv - \int v \, du$$

To compute $\int e^{3x} \cos 2x \, dx$, we can let $u = e^{3x}$, and $dv = \cos 2x \, dx$. It then follows that $du = 3e^{3x} dx$ and $v = \frac{1}{2} \sin 2x$. So we have

$$\int e^{3x} \cos 2x \, dx = (e^{3x}) \left(\frac{1}{2} \sin 2x \right) - \int \left(\frac{1}{2} \sin 2x \right) (3e^{3x}) \, dx + C$$

$$= \frac{1}{2} e^{3x} \sin 2x - \frac{3}{2} \int e^{3x} \sin 2x \, dx + C.$$

We now repeat this procedure to compute $\int e^{3x} \sin 2x \, dx$. We let $u = e^{3x}$, and $dv = \sin 2x \, dx$. It then follows that $du = 3e^{3x} dx$ and $v = -\frac{1}{2} \cos 2x$. So we have

$$\int e^{3x} \sin 2x \, dx = (e^{3x}) \left(-\frac{1}{2} \cos 2x \right) - \int \left(-\frac{1}{2} \cos 2x \right) (3e^{3x}) \, dx + C$$

$$= -\frac{1}{2} e^{3x} \cos 2x + \frac{3}{2} \int e^{3x} \cos 2x \, dx + C.$$

Putting these two results together, and dropping the constants (for now), we have

$$\int e^{3x} \cos 2x \, dx = \frac{1}{2} e^{3x} \sin 2x - \frac{3}{2} \int e^{3x} \sin 2x \, dx$$

$$= \frac{1}{2} e^{3x} \sin 2x - \frac{3}{2} \left(-\frac{1}{2} e^{3x} \cos 2x + \frac{3}{2} \int e^{3x} \cos 2x \, dx \right)$$

$$= \frac{1}{2} e^{3x} \sin 2x + \frac{3}{4} e^{3x} \cos 2x - \frac{9}{4} \int e^{3x} \cos 2x \, dx$$

Adding $\frac{9}{4}\int e^{3x}\cos 2x\,dx$ to each side of this equation gives

$$\frac{13}{4}\int e^{3x}\cos 2x\,dx = \frac{1}{2}e^{3x}\sin 2x + \frac{3}{4}e^{3x}\cos 2x.$$

Multiplying by $\frac{4}{13}$, and adding an arbitrary constant yields

$$\int e^{3x}\cos 2x\,dx = \frac{2}{13}e^{3x}\sin 2x + \frac{3}{13}e^{3x}\cos 2x + C.$$

(2) In the original solution above, we actually used **tabular integration by parts**. Note that this is a bit more sophisticated than the solution to problem 23.

In the first column we simply alternate signs starting with a plus sign.

In the middle column we put our choice for u, and we differentiate as we go down the column.

In the third column we put our choice for dv, and we integrate as we go down the column.

In this particular example we stop at the third row since the expression $\cos 2x$ appears for the second time in the third column.

Finally we follow the arrow pattern as seen in the original solution above to write down

$$\int e^{3x}\cos 2x\,dx = \frac{1}{2}e^{3x}\sin 2x + \frac{3}{4}e^{3x}\cos 2x - \frac{9}{4}\int e^{3x}\cos 2x\,dx.$$

From here we solve for $\int e^{3x}\cos 2x\,dx$.

LEVEL 3: SERIES

43. If g is a function such that $g'(x) = \cos(x^3)$, then the coefficient of x^{13} in the Maclaurin series for g is

   (A) $\frac{1}{13}$

   (B) $\frac{1}{24}$

   (C) $\frac{1}{52}$

   (D) $\frac{1}{312}$

   (E) $\frac{1}{720}$

111

Solution: The Maclaurin series for $\cos x$ is

$$\sum_{n=0}^{\infty} \frac{(-1)^n x^{2n}}{(2n)!} = 1 - \frac{x^2}{2!} + \frac{x^4}{4!} - \frac{x^6}{6!} + \cdots + \frac{(-1)^n x^{2n}}{(2n)!} + \cdots$$

So $g'(x) = \cos(x^3)$

$$= \sum_{n=0}^{\infty} \frac{(-1)^n x^{6n}}{(2n)!} = 1 - \frac{x^6}{2!} + \frac{x^{12}}{4!} - \frac{x^{18}}{6!} + \cdots + \frac{(-1)^n x^{6n}}{(2n)!} + \cdots$$

Therefore we have

$$g(x) = C + \sum_{n=0}^{\infty} \frac{(-1)^n x^{6n+1}}{(6n+1)(2n)!} = C + x - \frac{x^7}{7 \cdot 2!} + \frac{x^{13}}{13 \cdot 4!} - \frac{x^{19}}{19 \cdot 6!} + \cdots$$

where C is some constant.

So the coefficient of x^{13} is $\frac{1}{13 \cdot 4!} = \frac{1}{312}$, choice (D).

Notes: (1) See problem 32 for more information on Maclaurin series.

(2) It is worth memorizing the following Maclaurin series:

$$e^x = \sum_{n=0}^{\infty} \frac{x^n}{n!} = 1 + x + \frac{x^2}{2!} + \frac{x^3}{3!} + \frac{x^4}{4!} + \cdots + \frac{x^n}{n!} + \cdots$$

$$\cos x = \sum_{n=0}^{\infty} \frac{(-1)^n x^{2n}}{(2n)!} = 1 - \frac{x^2}{2!} + \frac{x^4}{4!} - \frac{x^6}{6!} + \cdots + \frac{(-1)^n x^{2n}}{(2n)!} + \cdots$$

$$\sin x = \sum_{n=0}^{\infty} \frac{(-1)^n x^{2n+1}}{(2n+1)!} = x - \frac{x^3}{3!} + \frac{x^5}{5!} - \frac{x^7}{7!} + \cdots + \frac{(-1)^n x^{2n+1}}{(2n+1)!} + \cdots$$

(3) If you forget the Maclaurin series for $f(x) = \cos x$, then you can find the series by using the definition. Recall that the **Maclaurin series** for the function f is

$$\sum_{n=0}^{\infty} \frac{f^n(0)}{n!} x^n = f(0) + f'(0)x + \frac{f''(0)}{2!} x^2 + \cdots + \frac{f^n(0)}{n!} x^n + \cdots$$

So $f(x) = \cos x$, $f'(x) = -\sin x$, $f''(x) = -\cos x$, $f'''(x) = \sin x$, $f^{(4)}(x) = \cos x$, ...

Notice that the derivatives just cycle through these four functions.

We now substitute 0 for x to get $f(0) = 1$, $f'(0) = 0$, $f''(0) = -1$, $f'''(0) = 0$, $f^{(4)}(0) = 1$, ...

Once again, we have a cyclical pattern. So using the definition of the Maclaurin series for f we get

$$\cos x = 1 + 0x - \frac{x^2}{2!} + \frac{0x^3}{3!} + \frac{x^4}{4!} + \frac{0x^5}{5!} - \frac{x^6}{6!} + \cdots + \frac{(-1)^n x^{2n}}{(2n)!} + \cdots$$

$$= 1 - \frac{x^2}{2!} + \frac{x^4}{4!} - \frac{x^6}{6!} + \cdots + \frac{(-1)^n x^{2n}}{(2n)!} + \cdots$$

(4) To get the Maclaurin series for $\cos x^3$, we simply replace x by x^3 in the Maclaurin series for $\cos x$.

(5) Taylor series, and more specifically, Maclaurin series, can be integrated term by term. Since an antiderivative of $a_n x^n$ is $\frac{a_n x^{n+1}}{n+1}$, it follows that the integral of

$$g'(x) = \cos(x^3) = 1 - \frac{x^6}{2!} + \frac{x^{12}}{4!} - \frac{x^{18}}{6!} + \cdots + \frac{(-1)^n x^{6n}}{(2n)!} + \cdots$$

is

$$g(x) = C + x - \frac{x^7}{7 \cdot 2!} + \frac{x^{13}}{13 \cdot 4!} - \frac{x^{19}}{19 \cdot 6!} + \cdots$$

where C is some constant. We do not need to know what C is to get the answer to this question.

44. For a series S, let

$$S = \frac{1}{\sqrt{3^3}} - \frac{1}{3} + \frac{1}{\sqrt{5^3}} - \frac{1}{9} + \frac{1}{\sqrt{7^3}} - \frac{1}{27} + \cdots + (-1)^n s_n + \cdots,$$

where $s_n = \begin{cases} \dfrac{1}{(n+2)^{\frac{3}{2}}} & \text{if } n \text{ is odd} \\ \dfrac{1}{3^{\frac{n}{2}}} & \text{if } n \text{ is even} \end{cases}$

Which of the following statements are true?

    I. S converges because the terms of S alternate in sign and $\lim_{n\to\infty} s_n = 0$.

    II. S diverges because the sequence (s_n) is not decreasing.

    III. S converges even though the sequence (s_n) is not decreasing.

(A) None
(B) I only
(C) II only
(D) III only
(E) I and III only

Solution: It is not sufficient that $\lim_{n\to\infty} s_n = 0$ for S to converge (in order to guarantee convergence, the sequence (s_n) must also be decreasing). So I is *not* true.

Note that the sequence (s_n) is actually *not* decreasing. For example, we have $s_1 = \frac{1}{(1+2)^{\frac{3}{2}}} = \frac{1}{3^{\frac{3}{2}}} \approx .192$, $s_2 = \frac{1}{3^{\frac{2}{2}}} = \frac{1}{3} \approx .333$, so that $s_1 < s_2$.

Now the series $T = \sum_{n=1}^{\infty} \frac{1}{n^{\frac{3}{2}}}$ is a p-series with $p = \frac{3}{2}$. Since $p > 1$, this series is convergent. The series A consisting of the odd terms of S form a series of positive terms with each term less than the corresponding term of T. It follows that A converges.

The series $B = \sum_{n=1}^{\infty} \left(\frac{1}{3}\right)^n$ is geometric with common ratio $r = \frac{1}{3}$. Since $r < 1$, this series is convergent.

Since A and B are both convergent series consisting of positive terms it follows that $A + B$ is convergent. Therefore S is absolutely convergent, thus convergent.

114

So S converges even though the sequence (s_n) is not decreasing. It follows that II is not true, and III is true. So the answer is choice (D).

Notes: (1) Recall that an **alternating series** has one of the forms $\sum_{n=1}^{\infty}(-1)^n a_n$ or $\sum_{n=1}^{\infty}(-1)^{n+1} a_n$ where $a_n > 0$ for each positive integer n.

The series S in this problem is an alternating series.

The **alternating series test** says that if (a_n) is a decreasing sequence with $\lim_{n\to\infty} a_n = 0$, then the alternating series converges.

The series S in this problem satisfies $\lim_{n\to\infty} s_n = 0$, but the sequence (s_n) is *not* decreasing. It follows that the alternating series test cannot be applied.

Note that the fact that the alternating series test cannot be applied does *not* tell us whether the series converges or diverges. We need to use a different method.

(2) See problem 30 for more information about p-series.

(3) See problems 11 and 14 for more information on geometric series.

(4) See problem 15 for more information on absolute convergence.

45. What is the approximation of the value e^5 obtained by the fifth-degree Taylor Polynomial about $x = 0$ for $f(x) = e^x$?

Solution: The fifth-degree Taylor Polynomial about $x = 0$ for $f(x) = e^x$ is $1 + x + \dfrac{x^2}{2!} + \dfrac{x^3}{3!} + \dfrac{x^4}{4!} + \dfrac{x^5}{5!}$.

So $e^5 \approx 1 + 5 + \dfrac{5^2}{2!} + \dfrac{5^3}{3!} + \dfrac{5^4}{4!} + \dfrac{5^5}{5!}$.

Notes: (1) See problem 31 for more information about Taylor Polynomials.

(2) See problem 43 (note (2)) for the Maclaurin series for e^x (remember that a Maclaurin series is the same thing as a Taylor series about $x = 0$).

The fifth-degree Taylor Polynomial about $x = 0$ for $f(x) = e^x$ is just the sum of the first six terms of the Maclaurin series for e^x.

46. * Using the Maclaurin Series for $\cos x$, approximate $\cos(0.3)$ to five decimal places.

Solution: The Maclaurin Series for $\cos x$ is

$$\sum_{n=0}^{\infty} \frac{(-1)^n x^{2n}}{(2n)!} = 1 - \frac{x^2}{2!} + \frac{x^4}{4!} - \frac{x^6}{6!} + \cdots + \frac{(-1)^n x^{2n}}{(2n)!} + \cdots$$

So $\cos(0.3) = 1 - \frac{(0.3)^2}{2!} + \frac{(0.3)^4}{4!} - \frac{(0.3)^6}{6!} + \cdots + \frac{(-1)^n (0.3)^{2n}}{(2n)!} + \cdots$

Since $\frac{(0.3)^6}{6!} \approx .000001 < .000005$, to five decimal place, we have
$\cos(0.3) \approx 1 - \frac{(0.3)^2}{2!} + \frac{(0.3)^4}{4!} = .9553375 \approx \mathbf{.95534}$.

Notes: (1) See problem 43 (note (2)) for the Maclaurin series for $\cos x$.

(2) The series representation for $\cos(0.3)$ is an alternating series that passes the alternating series test. Indeed, it is easy to see that the sequence $(\frac{(0.3)^{2n}}{(2n)!})$ is decreasing with limit 0.

(3) If the alternating series $\sum_{n=1}^{\infty}(-1)^n a_n$ or $\sum_{n=1}^{\infty}(-1)^{n+1} a_n$ converges by the alternating series test, then the sum of the first n terms is an approximation to the total sum of the series whose accuracy can be determined by the next term.

More precisely, $a_1 - a_2 + \cdots + (-1)^{n+1} a_n$ is an approximation to $\sum_{n=1}^{\infty}(-1)^{n+1} a_n$ whose error is less than or equal to a_{n+1}.

In this problem, $1 - \frac{(0.3)^2}{2!} + \frac{(0.3)^4}{4!}$ is an approximation of $\cos(0.3)$ whose error is less than $\frac{(0.3)^6}{6!}$.

(4) To guarantee that an approximation is accurate to five decimal places, we need the error to satisfy $|\text{error}| < .000005$.

Observe that there are five zeros after the decimal point.

In general to get an approximation accurate to n decimal places, there should be n zeros after the decimal point followed by a 5.

47. The Taylor series for a function g about $x = 2$ is given by $\sum_{n=1}^{\infty} \frac{(-1)^n 3^n}{n} (x-2)^n$ and converges to $g(x)$ for $|x - 2| < R$, where R is the radius of convergence of the Taylor series. Find R and the interval of convergence of the Taylor series.

Solution: We have

$$\lim_{n\to\infty}\left|\frac{\frac{(-1)^{n+1}\,3^{n+1}}{n+1}(x-2)^{n+1}}{\frac{(-1)^n\,3^n}{n}(x-2)^n}\right|=\lim_{n\to\infty}\frac{n}{n+1}\cdot 3|x-2|=3|x-2|.$$

$$3|x-2|<1 \text{ when } |x-2|<\tfrac{1}{3}.$$

So $R=\dfrac{1}{3}$.

Now, $|x-2|<\dfrac{1}{3}$ if and only if $-\dfrac{1}{3}<x-2<\dfrac{1}{3}$ if and only if $\dfrac{5}{3}<x<\dfrac{7}{3}$.

We still need to check the endpoints. When $x=\dfrac{7}{3}$, we get the convergent alternating series $\sum_{n=1}^{\infty}\dfrac{(-1)^n}{n}$, and when $x=\dfrac{5}{3}$ we get the divergent harmonic series $\sum_{n=1}^{\infty}\dfrac{1}{n}$. So the series converges for $\dfrac{5}{3}<x\le\dfrac{7}{3}$.

Therefore the interval of convergence is $(\tfrac{5}{3},\tfrac{7}{3}]$.

Notes: (1) The **Taylor series** for the function f about $x=a$ is

$$\sum_{n=0}^{\infty}\frac{f^n(a)}{n!}(x-a)^n$$

$$=f(a)+f'(a)(x-a)+\frac{f''(a)}{2!}(x-a)^2+\cdots+\frac{f^n(a)}{n!}(x-a)^n+\cdots$$

(2) A Taylor series is a special case of a power series. See problem 30 to learn how to find the radius of convergence and interval of convergence of a power series.

(3) See problem 12 for more information on the harmonic series and the alternating series test.

$$g(x)=\begin{cases}\dfrac{\sin x-x}{x^3} & \text{for } x\ne 0 \\ -\dfrac{1}{6} & \text{for } x=0\end{cases}$$

48. The function g, defined above, has derivatives of all orders. Write the first five nonzero terms and the general term for the Maclaurin series for g. Then determine whether g has a relative extremum at $x=0$. Justify your answer.

Solution: $\sin x = x - \dfrac{x^3}{3!} + \dfrac{x^5}{5!} - \dfrac{x^7}{7!} + \dfrac{x^9}{9!} - \dfrac{x^{11}}{11!} + \cdots + \dfrac{(-1)^n x^{2n+1}}{(2n+1)!} + \cdots$

So $\sin x - x = -\dfrac{x^3}{3!} + \dfrac{x^5}{5!} - \dfrac{x^7}{7!} + \dfrac{x^9}{9!} - \dfrac{x^{11}}{11!} + \cdots + \dfrac{(-1)^n x^{2n+1}}{(2n+1)!} + \cdots$

Therefore $g(x) = -\dfrac{1}{3!} + \dfrac{x^2}{5!} - \dfrac{x^4}{4!} + \dfrac{x^6}{9!} - \dfrac{x^8}{11!} + \cdots + \dfrac{(-1)^n x^{2n-2}}{(2n+1)!} + \cdots$

From the Maclaurin series for g we see that $g'(0) = 0$ and $\dfrac{g''(0)}{2!} = \dfrac{1}{5!}$, so that $g''(0) = \dfrac{2!}{5!} = \dfrac{1}{60} > 0$. So by the Second Derivative Test, g has a **relative minimum** at $x = 0$.

Notes: (1) See problem 32 for more information about Maclaurin series.

(2) See problem 43 (note (2)) for the Maclaurin series for $\sin x$.

(3) The **Second Derivative Test** says that if f is a differentiable function with $f'(c) = 0$, then

      (i) $f''(c) > 0 \Rightarrow f$ has a relative minimum at $x = c$.

      (ii) $f''(c) < 0 \Rightarrow f$ has a relative maximum at $x = c$.

Note that if $f''(c) = 0$, then the test cannot be used.

LEVEL 4: DIFFERENTIATION

49.   * Let r be the polar curve defined by $r(\theta) = 5\theta + \cos\theta$, where $0 \le \theta \le \pi$. A particle is travelling along r so that its position at time t is $\langle x(t), y(t)\rangle$ and such that $\dfrac{d\theta}{dt} = 3$. Find $\dfrac{dx}{dt}$ at the instant that $\theta = \dfrac{3\pi}{4}$, and interpret the meaning of your answer in the context of the problem.

Solution: $x = r(\theta)\cos\theta = (5\theta + \cos\theta)\cos\theta$.

$\dfrac{dx}{dt} = \dfrac{dx}{d\theta} \cdot \dfrac{d\theta}{dt} = [-(5\theta + \cos\theta)\sin\theta + (5 - \sin\theta)\cos\theta] \cdot \dfrac{d\theta}{dt}$.

So $\dfrac{dx}{dt}\Big|_{\theta = \frac{3\pi}{4}} = \left[-\left(\dfrac{15\pi}{4} - \dfrac{1}{\sqrt{2}}\right)\left(\dfrac{1}{\sqrt{2}}\right) + \left(5 - \dfrac{1}{\sqrt{2}}\right)\left(-\dfrac{1}{\sqrt{2}}\right)\right] \cdot 3$

$= 3\left(-\dfrac{15\pi}{4\sqrt{2}} + \dfrac{1}{2} - \dfrac{5}{\sqrt{2}} + \dfrac{1}{2}\right) = 3\left(-\dfrac{15\pi}{4\sqrt{2}} + \dfrac{4\sqrt{2}}{4\sqrt{2}} - \dfrac{20}{4\sqrt{2}}\right) = 3\left(\dfrac{4\sqrt{2} - 20 - 15\pi}{4\sqrt{2}}\right)$

$\approx -32.598.$

The x-coordinate of the particle is decreasing at a rate of 32.598.

Note: You should know the formulas for changing from polar to rectangular coordinates:

$$x = r \cos \theta \quad \text{and} \quad y = r \sin \theta.$$

50. * A particle moves along the curve defined by the equation $y = x^2 - x$. The x-coordinate of the particle satisfies $x(t) = \sqrt{7t + 2}$, for $t \geq 0$. Find the speed of the particle at time $t = 2$.

Solution: $\dfrac{dx}{dt} = \dfrac{7}{2\sqrt{7t+2}}$ and $\dfrac{dy}{dt} = \dfrac{dy}{dx} \cdot \dfrac{dx}{dt} = \dfrac{7(2x-1)}{2\sqrt{7t+2}}$.

When $t = 2$, $x(t) = 4$, $\dfrac{dx}{dt} = \dfrac{7}{8}$, and $\dfrac{dy}{dt} = \dfrac{49}{8}$.

Speed $= \sqrt{\left(\dfrac{dx}{dt}\right)^2 + \left(\dfrac{dy}{dt}\right)^2} = \sqrt{\left(\dfrac{7}{8}\right)^2 + \left(\dfrac{49}{8}\right)^2} \approx 6.187$.

Notes: (1) Here is an alternative method for finding $\dfrac{dy}{dt}$ at $t = 2$:

$$y(t) = \left(x(t)\right)^2 - x(t) = (7t + 2) - \sqrt{7t + 2}$$

So $\dfrac{dy}{dt} = 7 - \dfrac{7}{2\sqrt{7t+2}}$, and $\dfrac{dy}{dt}\Big|_{t=2} = 7 - \dfrac{7}{8} = \dfrac{49}{8}$.

(2) The speed of a particle with parametric equations $x = x(t)$, $y = y(t)$ is $\sqrt{\left(\dfrac{dx}{dt}\right)^2 + \left(\dfrac{dy}{dt}\right)^2}$

51. * A particle moves in the xy-plane so that its position at any time t, $0 \leq t \leq 2\pi$, is given by $x(t) = 2 \cos t$, $y(t) = e^{t^2} - t$. Find the acceleration vector at the time t when $x(t)$ attains its minimum value.

Solution: $x'(t) = -2 \sin t$ changes sign from negative to positive at $x = \pi$. Since $x = \pi$ is the only critical number of $x(t)$ in the interval $0 \leq t \leq 2\pi$, it follows that $x(t)$ attains its minimum value at $t = \pi$.

The position vector of the particle is $\langle 2 \cos t, e^{t^2} - t \rangle$. It follows that the velocity vector of the particle is $\langle -2 \sin t, 2te^{t^2} - 1 \rangle$, and so the acceleration vector of the particle is $\langle -2 \cos t, 4t^2 e^{t^2} + 2e^{t^2} \rangle$.

When $t = \pi$, the acceleration vector is $\langle 2, \left(4\pi^2 + 2\right)e^{\pi^2} \rangle$.

Notes: (1) See problem 35 for more information on the method used here to minimize $x(t)$.

(2) To differentiate a vector we simply differentiate each component separately. So the derivative of the vector $\langle x(t), y(t) \rangle$ is the vector $\langle x'(t), y'(t) \rangle$.

(3) Given a position vector $\langle x(t), y(t) \rangle$, the velocity vector is the derivative $\langle x'(t), y'(t) \rangle$, and the acceleration vector is the derivative of the velocity vector $\langle x''(t), y''(t) \rangle$.

52. The polar curve $r = f(\theta)$ satisfies $r > 0$ and $\frac{dr}{d\theta} < 0$ for $a < \theta < b$. What do these facts tell us about r? What do these facts tell us about the curve?

Solution: For $a < \theta < b$, the length of the radius r is decreasing. Therefore the curve gets closer to the origin as the angle θ increases from a to b.

LEVEL 4: INTEGRATION

53. * A particle moves in the xy-plane so that its velocity at any time t, $0 \leq t \leq 2\pi$, is given by $\frac{dx}{dt} = 2\cos t$, $\frac{dy}{dt} = e^{t^2} - t$. At time $t = 0$, the particle is at the point $(3,5)$. Find the y-coordinate of the position of the particle at time $t = 2$.

Solution: $y(2) = 5 + \int_0^2 (e^{t^2} - t)\, dt \approx \mathbf{19.453}$

Notes: (1) We do not need to worry about the particle changing direction in this problem since we only want the y-coordinate of the particle's position relative to its starting point.

(2) If we know the velocity vector $\langle \frac{dx}{dt}, \frac{dy}{dt} \rangle$ of a particle, then we can find its position vector $\langle x(t), y(t) \rangle$ by integrating each component of the velocity vector.

(3) $\int_a^b \frac{dy}{dt}\, dt = y(b) - y(a)$ gives the vertical distance between the position of the particle at time a and the position of the particle at time b.

So $\int_0^2 \frac{dy}{dt}\, dt$ is the vertical distance between the position of the particle at time 0 and the position of the particle at time 2.

120

Since the y-coordinate of the particle started at position $y(0) = 5$, we must add 5 to $\int_0^2 \frac{dy}{dt}\, dt$ to get the y-coordinate of the final position.

(4) We can compute $\int_0^2 (e^{t^2} - t)\, dt$ directly in our TI-84 calculator as follows:

Press MATH, followed by 9 (or scroll up 2 times and select 9:fnInt( ). Type e^(X^2) – X, X, 0, 2) followed by ENTER. The display will show 14.45262777.

(5) Remember to add 5 to get

$$5 + \int_0^2 (e^{t^2} - t)\, dt \;=\; 19.45262777.$$

We can then truncate this to **19.452** or round to **19.453** if we wish.

54. Let R be the region in the first and fourth quadrants bounded by the graph of $y = x^2 e^{x^3}$, the line $y = -3x$, and the vertical line $x = 2$. Write, but do not evaluate, an expression involving one or more integrals that gives the perimeter of R.

Solution: $\frac{d}{dx}\left[x^2 e^{x^3}\right] = 2x e^{x^3} + 3x^4 e^{x^3} = x e^{x^3}(2 + 3x^3)$. It follows that the perimeter of R is

$$\sqrt{2^2 + 6^2} + 6 + 4e^8 + \int_0^2 \sqrt{1 + \left[x e^{x^3}(2 + 3x^3)\right]^2}\, dx$$

$$= 2\sqrt{10} + 6 + 4e^8 + \int_0^2 \sqrt{1 + x^2 e^{2x^3}(2 + 3x^3)^2}\, dx$$

Notes: (1) Let's sketch the region

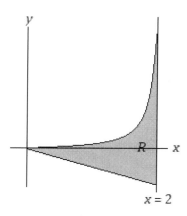

$x = 2$

(2) The perimeter of the region R given in the sketch is the sum of the lengths of the two line segments and the curve shown.

(3) The length of the vertical line segment is $2^2 e^{2^3} - (-3 \cdot 2) = 4e^8 + 6$

(4) The diagonal line segment passes through the points $(0,0)$ and $(2, -6)$. So we can use the distance formula to find its length:

$$\sqrt{2^2 + (-6)^2} = \sqrt{4 + 36} = \sqrt{40} = \sqrt{4 \cdot 10} = \sqrt{4}\sqrt{10} = 2\sqrt{10}.$$

(5) The length of the curve is given by the arc length formula:

$$\text{Arc length} = \int_a^b \sqrt{1 + \left(\frac{dy}{dx}\right)^2}\, dx = \int_0^2 \sqrt{1 + \left(\frac{dy}{dx}\right)^2}\, dx.$$

See problem 10 for more information on arc length.

55. The arc length for the graph of the differentiable function f between $x = 0$ and $x = 10$ is 4. Define the function h by $h(x) = \frac{f(2x)}{2}$. Find the arc length of the graph of $y = h(x)$ from $x = 0$ to $x = 5$.

Solution:

$$\text{Arc length of } h = \int_0^5 \sqrt{1 + \left(h'(x)\right)^2}\, dx = \int_0^5 \sqrt{1 + \left(f'(2x)\right)^2}\, dx$$

If we let $u = 2x$, then $du = 2dx$, and we have

$$\int_0^5 \sqrt{1 + \left(f'(2x)\right)^2}\, dx = \frac{1}{2}\int_0^{10} \sqrt{1 + \left(f'(u)\right)^2}\, du = \frac{1}{2}(4) = 2.$$

Note: See problem 10 for more information on computing arc length.

122

56. The average value of a function f on the unbounded interval $a \le x \le \infty$ is defined to be $\lim_{b \to \infty} \left[\frac{\int_a^b f(x)\,dx}{b-a} \right]$. Let h be the function given by $h(x) = \frac{2}{3\sqrt{x}}$. Show that the improper integral $\int_1^\infty h(x)\,dx$ diverges, but the average value of h on the interval $1 \le x \le \infty$ converges.

Solution: $\int_1^\infty h(x)\,dx = \int_1^\infty \frac{2}{3\sqrt{x}}\,dx = \frac{2}{3}\int_1^\infty x^{-\frac{1}{2}}\,dx = \frac{2}{3} \cdot 2x^{\frac{1}{2}} \Big|_1^\infty = \infty.$

$$\lim_{b \to \infty} \left[\frac{\int_1^b h(x)\,dx}{b-1} \right] = \lim_{b \to \infty} \left[\frac{\int_1^b \frac{2}{3\sqrt{x}}\,dx}{b-1} \right] = \lim_{b \to \infty} \left[\frac{\frac{4}{3}x^{\frac{1}{2}} \Big|_1^b}{b-1} \right]$$

$$= \frac{4}{3} \lim_{b \to \infty} \left(\frac{b^{\frac{1}{2}}-1}{b-1} \right) = \frac{4}{3} \cdot 0 = \mathbf{0}.$$

Notes: (1) See problem 7 for more information on this type of improper integral.

(2) To compute $\lim_{b \to \infty} \left(\frac{b^{\frac{1}{2}}-1}{b-1} \right)$, we can multiply both the numerator and denominator of the fraction under the limit by $\frac{1}{b}$ to get

$$\frac{b^{\frac{1}{2}}-1}{b-1} = \frac{\left(\frac{1}{b}\right)}{\left(\frac{1}{b}\right)} \cdot \frac{(b^{\frac{1}{2}}-1)}{(b-1)} = \frac{\frac{1}{\sqrt{b}}-\frac{1}{b}}{1-\frac{1}{b}}.$$

It follows that $\lim_{b \to \infty} \frac{b^{\frac{1}{2}}-1}{b-1} = \frac{\lim_{b \to \infty}\left(\frac{1}{\sqrt{b}}\right)-\lim_{b \to \infty}\left(\frac{1}{b}\right)}{\lim_{b \to \infty} 1-\lim_{b \to \infty}\left(\frac{1}{b}\right)} = \frac{0-0}{1-0} = \frac{0}{1} = 0.$

(3) L'Hôpital's rule can also be used to compute $\lim_{b \to \infty} \left(\frac{b^{\frac{1}{2}}-1}{b-1} \right)$ since the limit has the form $\frac{\infty}{\infty}$:

$$\lim_{b \to \infty} \frac{b^{\frac{1}{2}}-1}{b-1} = \lim_{b \to \infty} \frac{\frac{1}{2}b^{-\frac{1}{2}}}{1} = \lim_{b \to \infty} \frac{1}{2\sqrt{b}} = 0.$$

57. * A particle moves in the xy-plane so that its velocity at any time t, $0 \le t \le 2\pi$, is given by $\frac{dx}{dt} = 2\cos t$, $\frac{dy}{dt} = e^t - t$. Find the total distance traveled by the particle over the time interval $0 \le t \le 2\pi$.

123

Solution: Distance $= \int_0^{2\pi} \sqrt{(2 \cos t)^2 + (e^t - t)^2} \, dt \approx \mathbf{515.892}$

Notes: (1) The total distance traveled by a particle with parametric equations $x = x(t)$, $y = y(t)$, $a \le t \le b$ is equal to the arc length of the parametric curve from a to b.

(2) Recall that the **arc length** of the differentiable curve with parametric equations $x = x(t)$ and $y = y(t)$ from $t = a$ to $t = b$ is

$$\text{Arc length} = \int_a^b \sqrt{\left(\frac{dx}{dt}\right)^2 + \left(\frac{dy}{dt}\right)^2} \, dt$$

(3) See problem 53 to learn how to use your calculator to approximate the integral.

58. Consider the polar equations $r_1 = \sqrt{3}$ and $r_2 = 2 \sin \theta$. Let D be the region in the first quadrant bounded the graphs of the two equations and the y-axis. Set up an expression involving one or more integrals with respect to the polar angle θ that represents the area of D.

Solution: Area $= \dfrac{1}{2} \int_0^{\frac{\pi}{3}} (2 \sin \theta)^2 \, d\theta + \dfrac{1}{2} \int_{\frac{\pi}{3}}^{\frac{\pi}{2}} \left(\sqrt{3}\right)^2 \, d\theta$

Notes: (1) The graph of r_1 is a circle centered at the origin with radius $\sqrt{3}$, and the graph of r_2 is a circle centered at $(0,1)$ with radius 1 (see problem 24 to see how to sketch a polar graph in detail).

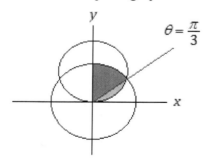

Observe that $r_1 = r_2$ when $\sqrt{3} = 2 \sin \theta$, or equivalently $\sin \theta = \frac{\sqrt{3}}{2}$. This gives $\theta = \frac{\pi}{3}$ in the first quadrant.

(3) Recall that the area of the polar curve $r(\theta)$ from $\theta = a$ to $\theta = b$ is $A = \dfrac{1}{2} \int_a^b r^2 \, d\theta$.

124

(4) The light gray region is the area of r_2 from $\theta = 0$ to $\theta = \frac{\pi}{3}$.

(5) The dark gray region is the area of r_1 from $\theta = \frac{\pi}{3}$ to $\theta = \frac{\pi}{2}$.

LEVEL 4: SERIES

59. A function h has derivatives of all orders at $x = 0$. Let $P_n(x)$ denote the nth-degree Taylor polynomial for h about $x = 0$. It is known that $h(0) = -2$, $h''(0) = -\frac{4}{5}$, $h'''(0) = \frac{5}{2}$, and $P_1\left(\frac{1}{4}\right) = -1$. Find $h'(0)$ and $P_3(x)$.

Solution: We have $P_1(x) = h(0) + h'(0)x = -2 + h'(0)x$. It follows that $-1 = P_1\left(\frac{1}{4}\right) = -2 + h'(0)\left(\frac{1}{4}\right)$. So $h'(0)\left(\frac{1}{4}\right) = -1 + 2 = 1$, and therefore $h'(0) = 1(4) = \mathbf{4}$.

$$P_3(x) = h(0) + h'(0)x + \frac{h''(0)x^2}{2!} + \frac{h'''(0)x^3}{3!} = -2 + 4x - \frac{4}{5} \cdot \frac{x^2}{2!} + \frac{5}{2} \cdot \frac{x^3}{3!}$$

$$= \mathbf{-2 + 4x - \frac{2}{5}x^2 + \frac{5}{12}x^3}.$$

Note: See problem 31 for more information about Taylor Polynomials.

60. The Taylor series for a function g about $x = 2$ is given by $\sum_{n=1}^{\infty} \frac{(-1)^n 3^n}{n}(x - 2)^n$ and converges to $g(x)$ for $|x - 2| < \frac{1}{3}$. Find the first four nonzero terms and the general term of the Taylor series for g', the derivative of g, about $x = 2$. Find the function g' to which the series converges for $|x - 2| < \frac{1}{3}$, and use this function to determine g for $|x - 2| < \frac{1}{3}$.

Solution: The first four terms of the Taylor series for g are

$$-3(x - 2) + \frac{9}{2}(x - 2)^2 - 9(x - 2)^3 + \frac{81}{4}(x - 2)^4.$$

It follows that the first four terms of the Taylor series for g' are

$$-3 + 9(x - 2) - 27(x - 2)^2 + 81(x - 2)^3.$$

The general term of the Taylor series for g' is

$$(-1)^n 3^n (x - 2)^{n-1} \text{ for } n \geq 1.$$

This series is geometric with common ratio $r = -3(x - 2)$.

So $g'(x) = \frac{-3}{1+3(x-2)} = \frac{-3}{3x-5} = \frac{3}{5-3x}$ for $|x - 2| < \frac{1}{3}$.

$g(x) = \int \frac{3}{5-3x} dx = -\ln|5 - 3x| + C$.

Since $g(2) = 0$, we have $0 = -\ln 1 + C = 0 + C = C$. So $C = 0$, and therefore $g(x) = -\ln|5 - 3x|$ for $|x - 2| < \frac{1}{3}$.

Note: See problem 47 for more information on Taylor series.

61. Write the first four nonzero terms of the Maclaurin series for $g(x) = \cos(x^2) + x^3 \sin x$. The find the value of $g^{(8)}(0)$.

Solution: $\cos x = 1 - \frac{x^2}{2!} + \frac{x^4}{4!} - \frac{x^6}{6!} + \cdots$

So $\cos(x^2) = 1 - \frac{x^4}{2!} + \frac{x^8}{4!} - \frac{x^{12}}{6!} + \cdots$

$\sin x = x - \frac{x^3}{3!} + \frac{x^5}{5!} - \frac{x^7}{7!} + \cdots$

So $x^3 \sin x = x^4 - \frac{x^6}{3!} + \frac{x^8}{5!} - \frac{x^{10}}{7!} + \cdots$

It follows that the first four terms of the desired Maclaurin series is

$$g(x) \approx 1 + \frac{x^4}{2} - \frac{x^6}{6} + \frac{6x^8}{5!}$$

$\frac{g^{(8)}(0)}{8!}$ is the coefficient of x^8 in the Maclaurin series for g. Therefore, we have $\frac{g^{(8)}(0)}{8!} = \frac{6}{5!}$. So $g^{(8)}(0) = \frac{6 \cdot 8!}{5!} = 6 \cdot 8 \cdot 7 \cdot 6 = \mathbf{2016}$.

Note: See problems 32 and 43 for the information on Maclaurin series needed in this problem.

62. Let $h(x) = \ln(1 + x^4)$. Write the first four nonzero terms of the Maclaurin series for $h'(x^2)$.

Solution: Let's begin by writing the first four nonzero terms of the Maclaurin series for $h(x) = \ln(1 + x)$.

$h'(x) = \frac{1}{1+x}$, $h''(x) = -\frac{1}{(1+x)^2}$, $h'''(x) = \frac{2}{(1+x)^3}$, and $h^{(4)}(x) = -\frac{3!}{(1+x)^4}$

So $h(0) = 0$, $h'(0) = 1$, $h''(0) = -1$, $h'''(0) = 2$, and $h^{(4)}(0) = -3!$

It follows that $\ln(1 + x) \approx x - \frac{x^2}{2} + \frac{x^3}{3} - \frac{x^4}{4}$. So

$$h(x) = \ln(1 + x^4) \approx x^4 - \frac{x^8}{2} + \frac{x^{12}}{3} - \frac{x^{16}}{4}$$

$$h'(x) \approx 4x^3 - 4x^7 + 4x^{11} - 4x^{15}$$

$$h'(x^2) \approx 4x^6 - 4x^{14} + 4x^{22} - 4x^{30}.$$

Note: See problems 32 and 43 for the information on Maclaurin series needed in this problem.

63. Let $h(x) = \ln(1 + x^4)$. Use the first two nonzero terms of the Maclaurin series for $g(x) = \int_0^x h'(u^2)\,du$ to approximate $g(1)$. Show that this approximation differs from $g(1)$ by less than $\frac{2}{11}$.

Solution: We have seen in the last problem that the Maclaurin series for $h'(u^2)$ is $4u^6 - 4u^{14} + 4u^{22} - 4u^{30} + \cdots + (-1)^{n+1}4u^{8n-2} + \cdots$

It follows that the Maclaurin series for $g(x)$ is

$$\frac{4x^7}{7} - \frac{4x^{15}}{15} + \frac{4x^{23}}{23} - \frac{4x^{31}}{31} + \cdots + \frac{(-1)^{n+1}4x^{8n-1}}{8n-1} + \cdots$$

So $g(1) \approx \frac{4}{7} - \frac{4}{15} = \frac{32}{105}$.

Note that the Maclaurin series for g at $x = 1$ is the alternating series

$$4\sum_{n=1}^{\infty} \frac{(-1)^{n+1}}{8n-1}$$

which converges by the alternating series test.

It follows that $g(1)$ exists, and $\left| g(1) - \frac{32}{105} \right| < \frac{4 \cdot 1^{23}}{23} = \frac{4}{23} < \frac{4}{22} = \frac{2}{11}$.

Notes: (1) See problems 32 and 43 for the information on Maclaurin series needed in this problem.

(2) See problem 46 for more information on approximating a Maclaurin series using the alternating series test remainder theorem.

127

$$g(x) = \begin{cases} \dfrac{\sin x - x}{x^3} & \text{for } x \neq 0 \\ -\dfrac{1}{6} & \text{for } x = 0 \end{cases}$$

64. The function g, defined above, has derivatives of all orders. Define the function h by $h(x) = 3 + \int_0^x g(u)\, du$. Write the fifth degree Taylor polynomial for h about $x = 0$, and then estimate the value of $h(1)$ to 4 decimal place accuracy.

Solution: $\sin x = x - \dfrac{x^3}{3!} + \dfrac{x^5}{5!} - \dfrac{x^7}{7!} + \dfrac{x^9}{9!} - \dfrac{x^{11}}{11!} + \cdots + \dfrac{(-1)^n x^{2n+1}}{(2n+1)!} + \cdots$

So $\sin x - x = -\dfrac{x^3}{3!} + \dfrac{x^5}{5!} - \dfrac{x^7}{7!} + \dfrac{x^9}{9!} - \dfrac{x^{11}}{11!} + \cdots + \dfrac{(-1)^n x^{2n+1}}{(2n+1)!} + \cdots$

Therefore $g(x) = -\dfrac{1}{3!} + \dfrac{x^2}{5!} - \dfrac{x^4}{7!} + \dfrac{x^6}{9!} - \dfrac{x^8}{11!} + \cdots + \dfrac{(-1)^n x^{2n-2}}{(2n+1)!} + \cdots$

The fifth degree Taylor polynomial for h about $x = 0$ is

$$P_5(x) = 3 - \frac{x}{3!} + \frac{x^3}{3 \cdot 5!} - \frac{x^5}{5 \cdot 7!}$$

Since $\dfrac{1^5}{5 \cdot 7!} \approx .00003 < .00005$, and the Maclaurin series for h evaluated at $x = 1$ is an alternating series whose terms decrease in absolute value to 0, we have $|h(1) - P_3(1)| < .00005$. So to 4 decimal place accuracy we have $g(1) = P_3(1) = 3 - \dfrac{1}{3!} + \dfrac{1}{3 \cdot 5!} = \mathbf{2.8361}$.

Notes: (1) See problems 32 and 43 for the information on Maclaurin series needed in this problem.

(2) See problem 46 for more information on approximating a Maclaurin series using the alternating series test remainder theorem.

128

* 65 – 70 For $t \geq 0$, a particle is moving along a curve so that its position at time t is $(x(t), y(t))$. At time $t = 1$, the particle is at position (3,5). It is known that $\frac{dx}{dt} = \cos^2 t$ and $\frac{dy}{dt} = \frac{e^t}{\sqrt{t+3}}$.

65. * Is the vertical movement of the particle upward or downward at time $t = 1$? Justify your answer. Find the slope of the path of the particle at time $t = 1$.

Solution: $\frac{dy}{dt}\big|_{t=1} = \frac{e^1}{\sqrt{1+3}} = \frac{e}{2} > 0$. So the particle is moving **up** at time $t = 1$.

$\frac{dx}{dt}\big|_{t=1} = \cos^2 1$ and so $\frac{dy}{dx}\big|_{t=1} = \frac{\frac{dy}{dt}\big|_{t=1}}{\frac{dx}{dt}\big|_{t=1}} = \frac{e}{2\cos^2 1} \approx 4.655$ or 4.656.

66. * Find the x-coordinate of the particle's position at time $t = \frac{\pi}{2}$.

Solution: $x\left(\frac{\pi}{2}\right) = 3 + \int_1^{\frac{\pi}{2}} \cos^2 t \, dt \approx 3.058$.

67. * Find the speed of the particle at time $t = \frac{\pi}{2}$.

Solution: Speed $= \sqrt{\left(x'\left(\frac{\pi}{2}\right)\right)^2 + \left(y'\left(\frac{\pi}{2}\right)\right)^2} = \sqrt{0^2 + \left(\frac{e^{\frac{\pi}{2}}}{\sqrt{\frac{\pi}{2}+3}}\right)^2}$

$$= \frac{e^{\frac{\pi}{2}}}{\sqrt{\frac{\pi}{2}+3}} \approx 2.250 = 2.25.$$

68. * Find the acceleration vector of the particle at time $t = \frac{\pi}{2}$.

Solution: $x''(t) = -2\cos t \sin t$ and so $x''\left(\frac{\pi}{2}\right) = -2(0)(1) = 0$

$y''(t) = \frac{\sqrt{t+3}\,e^t - \frac{e^t}{2\sqrt{t+3}}}{t+3}$ and so $y''\left(\frac{\pi}{2}\right) = \frac{\sqrt{\frac{\pi}{2}+3}\cdot e^{\frac{\pi}{2}} - \frac{e^{\frac{\pi}{2}}}{2\sqrt{\frac{\pi}{2}+3}}}{\frac{\pi}{2}+3} \approx 2.004$

Acceleration $= \langle x''\left(\frac{\pi}{2}\right), y''\left(\frac{\pi}{2}\right)\rangle = \langle 0, 2.004\rangle$.

69. * Find the distance traveled by the particle from time $t = 1$ to $t = \frac{\pi}{2}$.

Solution: Distance $= \int_1^{\frac{\pi}{2}} \sqrt{(x'(t))^2 + \left(y'(t)\right)^2} \, dt$

$$= \int_1^{\frac{\pi}{2}} \sqrt{(\cos^2 t)^2 + \left(\frac{et}{\sqrt{t+3}}\right)^2} \, dt \approx \mathbf{1.012}.$$

70. * Find the time t, $0 \le t \le 2$, when the line tangent to the path of the particle is vertical. Is the direction of the motion of the particle upward or downward at that time. Justify your answer.

Solution: $\frac{dx}{dt} = 0$ when $\cos^2 t = 0$. On the interval $0 \le t \le 2$, this happens when $t = \frac{\pi}{2}$.

Since $y'\left(\frac{\pi}{2}\right) = \frac{e^{\frac{\pi}{2}}}{\sqrt{\frac{\pi}{2}+3}} > 0$, the particle is moving **upward** at time $t = \frac{\pi}{2}$.

71 – 76 The polar curves r_1 and r_2 are given by $r_1(\theta) = 4$ and $r_2(\theta) = 4 - 3\sin(2\theta)$.

71. Sketch the graphs of r_1 and r_2 for $0 \le \theta \le \pi$, and shade the region D that is inside both the graphs of r_1 and r_2.

Solution:

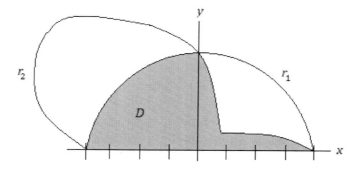

Note: See problem 24 to see how to sketch a polar graph in detail

130

72. Find the area of the region D that is inside both the graphs of r_1 and r_2 for $0 \le \theta \le \pi$.

Solution: Area $= \frac{16\pi}{4} + \frac{1}{2}\int_0^{\frac{\pi}{2}}(4 - 3\sin(2\theta))^2 \, d\theta$

$= 4\pi + \frac{1}{2}\int_0^{\frac{\pi}{2}}(16 - 24\sin(2\theta) + \frac{9}{2}(1 - \cos(4\theta))) \, d\theta$

$= 4\pi + \frac{1}{2}\left(16\theta + 12\cos(2\theta) + \frac{9}{2}(\theta - \frac{1}{4}\sin(4\theta))\right) \Big|_0^{\frac{\pi}{2}}$

$= 4\pi + (\frac{41\pi}{8} - 12) = \frac{73\pi}{8} - \textbf{12}.$

Note: If a calculator were allowed we could just write down the decimal approximation **16.667**. See problem 53 to learn how to use your calculator to approximate the integral.

73. For the curve r_2, find the value of $\frac{dy}{d\theta}$ at $\theta = \frac{\pi}{3}$.

Solution: $y = r_2 \sin\theta = (4 - 3\sin(2\theta))\sin\theta$.

So $\frac{dy}{d\theta} = (4 - 3\sin(2\theta))\cos\theta - 6\cos(2\theta)\sin\theta$.

Therefore $\frac{dy}{d\theta}\Big|_{\theta=\frac{\pi}{3}} = \left(4 - 3\sin\left(\frac{2\pi}{3}\right)\right)\cos\frac{\pi}{3} - 6\cos\left(\frac{2\pi}{3}\right)\sin\frac{\pi}{3}$

$= \left(4 - \frac{3\sqrt{3}}{2}\right)\left(\frac{1}{2}\right) - 6\left(-\frac{1}{2}\right)\left(\frac{\sqrt{3}}{2}\right) = 2 - \frac{3\sqrt{3}}{4} + \frac{6\sqrt{3}}{4} = \textbf{2} + \frac{3\sqrt{3}}{4}.$

Note: If a calculator were allowed we could just write down the decimal approximation **3.299**. See problem 2 to learn how to use your calculator to approximate the derivative.

74. The distance between r_1 and r_2 changes for $0 < \theta < \frac{\pi}{2}$. Find the rate at which the distance between the two curves is changing with respect to θ when $\theta = \frac{\pi}{6}$.

Solution: The distance between r_1 and r_2 is

$$D = 4 - (4 - 3\sin(2\theta)) = 3\sin(2\theta).$$

So $\frac{dD}{d\theta} = 6\cos(2\theta)$, and therefore $\frac{dD}{d\theta}\Big|_{\theta=\frac{\pi}{6}} = 6\cos\frac{\pi}{3} = 6\left(\frac{1}{2}\right) = \textbf{3}.$

131

75. A particle moves along the curve r_2 so that $\frac{d\theta}{dt} = 4$ for all times $t \geq 0$. Find the value of $\frac{dr_2}{dt}$ at $\theta = \frac{\pi}{6}$.

Solution: $\frac{dr_2}{dt} = \frac{dr_2}{d\theta} \cdot \frac{d\theta}{dt} = \frac{dr_2}{d\theta} \cdot 4$.

Also, $\frac{dr_2}{d\theta} = -6\cos(2\theta)$, so that $\frac{dr_2}{d\theta}\big|_{\theta=\frac{\pi}{6}} = -6\cos\left(\frac{\pi}{3}\right) = -3$.

So $\frac{dr_2}{dt}\big|_{\theta=\frac{\pi}{6}} = (-3)(4) = -12$.

76. * A particle moves along the curve r_2 so that at time t, $\theta = t^3$. Find the times t in the interval $2 \leq t \leq 2.5$ for which the y-coordinate of the particle's position is -3. Then find the particle's position and velocity vectors in terms of t.

Solution: $y = r_2 \sin\theta$. So $y(\theta) = (4 - 3\sin(2\theta)) \sin\theta$.

$y(t) = (4 - 3\sin(2t^3)) \sin(t^3)$ and $y(t) = -3$ when $t \approx \mathbf{2.213}$ and $t \approx \mathbf{2.295}$.

Now, $x = r_2 \cos\theta$. So $x(\theta) = (4 - 3\sin(2\theta)) \cos\theta$.

$x(t) = (4 - 3\sin(2t^3)) \cos(t^3)$.

Position vector $= \langle x(t), y(t) \rangle$

$$= \langle (\mathbf{4 - 3\sin(2t^3)}) \cos(t^3), (\mathbf{4 - 3\sin(2t^3)}) \sin(t^3) \rangle.$$

Velocity vector $= \langle x'(t), y'(t) \rangle =$

$$\langle -3t^2\sin(t^3)(4 - 3\sin(2t^3)) - 18t^2\cos(2t^3)\cos(t^3),$$
$$3t^2\cos(t^3)(4 - 3\sin(2t^3)) - 18t^2\cos(2t^3)\sin(t^3) \rangle$$

Note: You will need to use the graphing features of your calculator to determine when $y(t) = -3$. We graph $(4 - 3\sin(2t^3)) \sin(t^3)$ and -3 in our calculator in the window $[2,2.5] \times [-5,5]$ and use the "intersect" feature twice to find that $t \approx \mathbf{2.213}$ and $t \approx \mathbf{2.295}$.

132

77 – 80 The function g has a Taylor series about $x = 3$ that converges to $g(x)$ for all x in the interval of convergence. The nth derivative of g at $x = 3$ is given by $g^{(n)}(3) = \frac{(n+2)!}{5^n}$ for $n \geq 1$, and $g(3) = 2$.

77. Write the first four terms and the general term of the Taylor series for g about $x = 3$.

Solution: $g(3) = 2$, $g'(3) = \frac{3!}{5}$, $g''(3) = \frac{4!}{5^2}$, $g'''(3) = \frac{5!}{5^3}$. So

$$g(x) = g(3) + g'(3)(x - 3) + \frac{g''(3)}{2!}(x - 3)^2 + \frac{g'''(3)}{3!}(x - 3)^3 + \cdots$$
$$+ \frac{g^{(n)}(3)}{n!}(x - 3)^n + \cdots$$

$$= 2 + \frac{3!}{5}(x - 3) + \frac{4!}{5^2(2!)}(x - 3)^2 + \frac{5!}{5^3(3!)}(x - 3)^3 + \cdots$$
$$+ \frac{(n + 2)!}{5^n(n!)}(x - 3)^n + \cdots$$

$$= 2 + \frac{3 \cdot 2}{5}(x - 3) + \frac{4 \cdot 3}{5^2}(x - 3)^2 + \frac{5 \cdot 4}{5^3}(x - 3)^3 + \cdots$$
$$+ \frac{(n + 2)(n + 1)}{5^n}(x - 3)^n + \cdots$$

or $\sum_{n=0}^{\infty} \frac{(n+2)(n+1)}{5^n}(x - 3)^n$.

Note: See problem 47 for more information on Taylor series.

78. Find the radius of convergence for the Taylor series for g about $x = 3$. Justify your answer.

Solution: We have

$$\lim_{n\to\infty} \left| \frac{\frac{(n+3)(n+2)}{5^{n+1}}(x-3)^{n+1}}{\frac{(n+2)(n+1)}{5^n}(x-3)^n} \right| = \lim_{n\to\infty} \frac{n^2+5n+6}{n^2+3n+2} \cdot \frac{1}{5}|x - 3| = \frac{1}{5}|x - 3|.$$

$$\frac{1}{5}|x - 3| < 1 \text{ when } |x - 3| < 5.$$

So the radius of convergence is **5**.

Note: See problems 15, 16 and 30 for more information on the ratio test, power series, and radius of convergence.

133

79. Find the interval of convergence for the Taylor series for g about $x = 3$. Justify your answer.

Solution: We have $|x - 3| < 5$. This is equivalent to $-5 < x - 3 < 5$ or $-2 < x < 8$.

When $x = 8$, the series is $\sum_{n=0}^{\infty} \frac{(n+2)(n+1)}{5^n} 5^n = \sum_{n=0}^{\infty} (n + 2)(n + 1)$ which diverges by the divergence test.

When $x = -2$, the series is $\sum_{n=0}^{\infty} (-1)^n (n + 2)(n + 1)$ which also diverges by the divergence test.

It follows that the interval of convergence is $(-2, 8)$.

80. Let G be a function satisfying $G(3) = 1$ and $G'(x) = g(x)$ for all x. Write the first four terms and the general term of the Taylor series for G about $x = 3$. Does this Taylor series converge at $x = -3$?

Solution: $G(3) = 1$, $G'(3) = g(3)$, $G''(3) = g'(3)$, $G'''(3) = g''(3)$.

$$G(x) = G(3) + g(3)(x - 3) + \frac{g'(3)}{2!}(x - 3)^2 + \frac{g''(3)}{3!}(x - 3)^3 + \cdots$$
$$+ \frac{g^{(n-1)}(3)}{n!}(x - 3)^n + \cdots$$

$$= 1 + 2(x - 3) + \frac{3!}{5(2!)}(x - 3)^2 + \frac{4!}{5^2(3!)}(x - 3)^3 + \cdots$$
$$+ \frac{(n + 1)!}{5^{n-1}(n!)}(x - 3)^n + \cdots$$

$$= 1 + 2(x - 3) + \frac{3}{5}(x - 3)^2 + \frac{4}{5^2}(x - 3)^3 + \cdots + \frac{(n+1)}{5^{n-1}}(x - 3)^n + \cdots$$

The radius of convergence of this series is $R = 5$. Since we have $|-3 - 3| = |-6| = 6 > 5$, it follows that this Taylor series does not converge at $x = -3$.

134

SUPPLEMENTAL BC PROBLEMS
QUESTIONS

LEVEL 1: DIFFERENTIATION

1. $\dfrac{d}{dx}\left[\dfrac{x \arctan \sqrt{x}}{3}\right] =$

2. If $h(x) = \sqrt{\sqrt{x} + x}$, then $h'(1) =$

3. If $x = \sin^{-1}(t^2)$ and $y = e^{3\ln t}$, then $\dfrac{dy}{dx} =$

4. If $\mathbf{G}$ is the vector-valued function defined by $\mathbf{G}(t) = \langle \dfrac{1+t^3}{1+t}, \cos^2 t - \sin^2 t \rangle$, then $\mathbf{G}''(0) =$

LEVEL 1: INTEGRATION

5. $\int_{-3}^{1} \dfrac{|x|}{x} dx =$

6. * If the function h given by $h(x) = \dfrac{\ln x}{x}$ has an average value of $\dfrac{1}{4}$ on the interval $[1, b]$, then $b =$

7. $\int_{0}^{\infty} \dfrac{\arctan x}{x^2+1} dx$ is

8. Let $y = f(x)$ be the solution to the differential equation $\dfrac{dy}{dx} = \ln(xy)$ with the initial condition $f(1) = 1$. What is the approximation of $f(2)$ if Euler's method is used, starting at $x = 1$ with a step size of 0.5?

9. * What is the area of the closed region bounded by the curve $y = \arctan x$, and the lines $x = -2$ and $y = -\dfrac{\pi}{4}$?

10. Find the length of the graph of $y = 2\left(x - \dfrac{1}{9}\right)^{3/2}$ between $x = 1$ and $x = 4$?

11. The sum of the infinite geometric series $\frac{1}{3} + \frac{4}{15} + \frac{16}{75} + \cdots$ is

12. Which of the following series converge?

    I. $\sum_{n=1}^{\infty} \frac{(-3)^n}{n}$

    II. $\sum_{n=1}^{\infty} \frac{e^n}{2e^n + 5}$

    III. $\sum_{n=1}^{\infty} \frac{1}{n^{\frac{3}{2}}}$

    (A) I only
    (B) II only
    (C) III only
    (D) I and III only
    (E) II, and III only

13. If $\lim_{b \to \infty} \int_1^b \frac{1}{x^p} \, dx = \infty$, then which of the following must be true?

    (A) $\sum_{n=1}^{\infty} \frac{1}{n^{p+1}}$ diverges

    (B) $\sum_{n=1}^{\infty} \frac{1}{n^p}$ converges

    (C) $\sum_{n=1}^{\infty} \frac{1}{n^p}$ diverges

    (D) $\sum_{n=1}^{\infty} \frac{1}{n^{p-1}}$ converges

    (E) $\sum_{n=1}^{\infty} \frac{1}{n^{p-2}}$ converges

136

14. Which of the following series converge to $-\frac{5}{4}$?

I. $\sum_{n=1}^{\infty} \frac{5}{(-3)^n}$

II. $\sum_{n=1}^{\infty} \frac{1-\sqrt{n}}{3\sqrt{n}+2}$

III. $\sum_{n=1}^{\infty} \frac{1}{\sqrt{n}}$

(A) I only
(B) II only
(C) III only
(D) I and III only
(E) II, and III only

15. Which of the following series diverge?

I. $\sum_{n=1}^{\infty} \frac{n^3-n+1}{\ln n}$

II. $\sum_{n=1}^{\infty} (\frac{101}{100})^n$

III. $\sum_{n=1}^{\infty} \frac{n!}{3^n}$

(A) I only
(B) II only
(C) III only
(D) I and III only
(E) I, II, and III

16. What are all values of x for which the series $\sum_{n=1}^{\infty} \frac{(-3)^n x^n}{n^2+1}$ converges?

LEVEL 2: DIFFERENTIATION

17. Write an equation of the normal line to the curve $y = \sqrt{\ln x}$ at the point $(e, 1)$.

18. A curve is described by the parametric equations $x = \cos t$ and $y = e^{\sqrt{\sin t}}$. An equation of the line tangent to the curve at the point where $t = \frac{\pi}{2}$ is

19. * The line perpendicular to the tangent line to the curve represented by the equation $y = \ln \sqrt{x}$ at the point $(e^2, 1)$ also intersects the curve at $x =$

20. If $\frac{d}{dx}[k(x)] = h(x)$ and if $g(x) = 2x^3 - 5$, then $\frac{d}{dx}[g(k(x))] =$

    (A) $6(h(x))(k(x))^2$

    (B) $6(h(x))(k(x))^2 - 5h(x)$

    (C) $h'(x)$

    (D) $6x^2 h(x)$

    (E) $h(2x^3 - 5)$

LEVEL 2: INTEGRATION

21. $\int_0^3 \frac{dx}{\sqrt{3-x}} =$

22. Find the length of $y = \ln(\sec x)$ between $x = 0$ and $x = \frac{\pi}{4}$?

23. $\int x^2 e^x dx =$

24. The area enclosed by the graph of the polar equation $r = 2\cos(3\theta)$ is

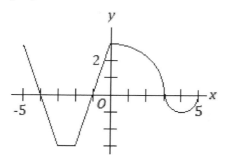

25. Let g be the continuous function defined on $[-5,5]$ whose graph, consisting of three line segments, a quarter circle centered at the origin, and a semicircle centered at $(4,0)$, is shown above. If $G(x) = \int_0^x g(t)\, dt$, where is $G(x)$ negative?

138

26. Find the length of the arc of the curve defined by $x(t) = 5 \sin t$ and $y(t) = 5 \cos t$, from $t = 0$ to $t = 2\pi$.

LEVEL 2: SERIES

27. If $\sum_{n=2}^{\infty} \frac{\ln n}{n} =$

 (A) $\ln(\ln 2)$

 (B) $\frac{\ln 2}{2}$

 (C) $\ln 2$

 (D) $\frac{1}{\ln 2}$

 (E) The series diverges.

28. If $g(x) = \sum_{n=1}^{\infty}(\cos^2 x)^n$, then $g\left(\frac{\pi}{6}\right) =$

29. $\sum_{n=1}^{\infty}\left(\frac{5^n}{(4+n^2)^{80}}\right)\left(\frac{(3+n^2)^{80}}{5^{n+1}}\right) =$

 (A) $\frac{1}{5}$

 (B) $\frac{1}{4}$

 (C) $\frac{1}{3}$

 (D) $\frac{3}{4}$

 (E) The series diverges.

30. Find the interval of convergence for the series $\sum_{n=1}^{\infty}\frac{(x-5)^n}{\sqrt{n}(2^n)}$.

31. The third-degree Taylor polynomial about $x = 0$ of $\ln(3 - 3x)$ is

32. If $\sum_{n=0}^{\infty} a_n x^n$ is a Maclaurin series that converges to $g(x)$ for all x. then $g''(-1) =$

 (A) -1
 (B) $-a_2$
 (C) $\sum_{n=2}^{\infty}(-1)^n a_n$
 (D) $\sum_{n=2}^{\infty}(-1)^n n(n-1)a_n$
 (E) $\sum_{n=2}^{\infty}(-1)^n n(n-1)a_n^{n-2}$

139

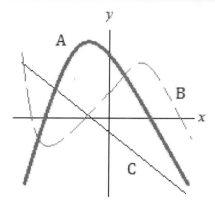

33. Three graphs labeled A, B, and C are shown above. One is the graph of f, one is the graph of f', and one is the graph of f''. When $f''(x) = 0$, what can we say about $f(x)$ and $f'(x)$?

    (A) $f(x) > 0$ and $f'(x) > 0$
    (B) $f(x) > 0$ and $f'^{(x)} < 0$
    (C) $f(x) < 0$ and $f'(x) > 0$
    (D) $f(x) < 0$ and $f'^{(x)} < 0$
    (E) $f(x)$ and $f'(x)$ have opposite signs

34. A point (x,y) is moving along the curve $y = f(x)$. At the instant when the slope of the curve is $\frac{3}{7}$, the y-coordinate of the point is increasing at the rate of 5 units per minute. The rate of change, in units per minute, of the x-coordinate of the point is

35. Let h be a differentiable function whose domain is the open interval (a, b). The graph of h'' has exactly one relative minimum and one relative maximum. Which of the following must be true?

    (A) The graph of h has 1 point of inflection
    (B) The graph of h' has 1 points of inflection
    (C) The graph of h has 2 points of inflection
    (D) The graph of h' has 2 points of inflection
    (E) h' has 2 critical numbers

36. * Let K be defined by $K(t) = 3\cos\left(\frac{\pi t}{5}\right) - 8\sin\left(\frac{\pi t}{6}\right) + 45$. For $0 \le t \le 10$, K is increasing most rapidly when $t =$

LEVEL 3: INTEGRATION

37. $\int \frac{x+13}{x^2-4x-5} dx =$

   (A) $\ln|(x-5)(x+1)| + C$
   (B) $\ln|(x-5)^2(x+1)^3| + C$
   (C) $\ln|(x-5)^3(x+1)^2| + C$
   (D) $\ln\left|\frac{(x-5)^3}{(x+1)^2}\right| + C$
   (E) $\ln\left|\frac{(x+1)^2}{(x-5)^3}\right| + C$

38. * Let G be defined by $G(x) = \int_3^x (7-t^2)\ln(t^2-5)\, dt$, Which of the following statements about G must be true?

   I. G is increasing on $(3,4)$.
   II. G is concave up on $(3,4)$
   III. $G(5) > 0$

   (A) None
   (B) I only
   (C) II only
   (D) III only
   (E) I, II and III

39. A solid has a rectangular base that lies in the first quadrant and is bounded by the x- and y-axes and the lines $x = 5$ and $y = 1$. The height of the solid above the point (x,y) is $x\ln(x+1)$. Which of the following is a Riemann sum approximation for the volume of the solid?

   (A) $\sum_{i=1}^n \frac{25i^2}{n^2}\ln(\frac{5i+n}{n})$
   (B) $\sum_{i=1}^n \frac{25i}{n^2}\ln(\frac{5i+n}{n})$
   (C) $\sum_{i=1}^n \frac{5i}{n^2}\ln(\frac{5i+n}{n})$
   (D) $\sum_{i=1}^n \frac{5}{n}\ln(\frac{5i+n}{n})$
   (E) $\sum_{i=1}^n \frac{1}{n}\ln(\frac{5i+n}{n})^2$

141

x	$f'(x)$
-4	0
-3.5	2
-3	1
-2.5	4
-2	3
-1.5	6
-1	5

40. The table above gives selected values for the derivative of a function f on the interval $-4 \le x \le -1$. If $f(-4) = 1$ and Euler's method with a step size of 1 is used to approximate $f(-1)$, what is the resulting approximation?

41. Find the area in the first quadrant between the outer envelope and the smaller loop of the graph of $r = 2 + 4\cos\theta$.

42. $\int e^{2x} \sin 3x \, dx =$

LEVEL 3: SERIES

43. If g is a function such that $g'(x) = e^{x^3}$, then the coefficient of x^{10} in the Maclaurin series for g is

44. For a series S, let

$$S = \frac{1}{\sqrt{5^5}} - \frac{1}{5} + \frac{1}{\sqrt{7^5}} - \frac{1}{25} + \frac{1}{\sqrt{9^5}} - \frac{1}{125} + \cdots + (-1)^n s_n + \cdots,$$

$$\text{where } s_n = \begin{cases} \dfrac{1}{(n+4)^{\frac{5}{2}}} & \text{if } n \text{ is odd} \\[2mm] \dfrac{1}{5^{\frac{n}{2}}} & \text{if } n \text{ is even} \end{cases}$$

Which of the following statements are true?

    I. S converges because the terms of S alternate in sign and $\lim_{n \to \infty} s_n = 0$.

    II. S diverges because the sequence (s_n) is not decreasing.

    III. S converges even though the sequence (s_n) is not decreasing.

    (A) None
    (B) I only
    (C) II only
    (D) III only
    (E) I and III only

45. What is the approximation of the value $\cos 5$ obtained by the sixth-degree Taylor Polynomial about $x = 0$ for $(x) = \cos x$?.

46. * Using the Maclaurin Series for $\sin x$, approximate $\sin(0.3)$ to four decimal places.

47. The Taylor series for a function g about $x = 3$ is given by $\sum_{n=1}^{\infty} \frac{(-1)^n 4^n}{n^2} (x-3)^n$ and converges to $g(x)$ for $|x - 3| < R$, where R is the radius of convergence of the Taylor series. Find R and the interval of convergence of the Taylor series.

$$h(x) = \begin{cases} \dfrac{\cos x - 1}{x} & \text{for } x \neq 0 \\ 0 & \text{for } x = 0 \end{cases}$$

48. The function h, defined above, has derivatives of all orders. Write the first five nonzero terms and the general term for the Maclaurin series for h. Then determine whether h has a relative extremum at $x = 0$. Justify your answer.

LEVEL 4: DIFFERENTIATION

49. * Let r be the polar curve defined by $r(\theta) = 7e^{\frac{6}{7}\theta} + \sin 2\theta$, where $0 \leq \theta \leq 2\pi$. A particle is travelling along r so that its position at time t is $\langle x(t), y(t) \rangle$ and such that $\dfrac{d\theta}{dt} = 2$. Find $\dfrac{dy}{dt}$ at the instant that $\theta = \dfrac{7\pi}{6}$, and interpret the meaning of your answer in the context of the problem.

50. * A particle moves along the curve defined by the equation $y = \ln(x^2 + 1)$. The x-coordinate of the particle satisfies $x(t) = \sqrt{t - 1}$, for $t \geq 1$. Find the speed of the particle at time $t = 5$.

51. * A particle moves in the xy-plane so that its position at any time t, $0 \leq t \leq 2\pi$, is given by $x(t) = 5\sin\frac{t}{2}$, $y(t) = \ln 5t$. Find the acceleration vector at the time t when $x(t)$ attains its maximum value.

52. The polar curve $r = f(\theta)$ satisfies $r > 0$ and $\dfrac{dr}{d\theta} > 0$ for $a < \theta < b$. What do these facts tell us about r? What do these facts tell us about the curve?

LEVEL 4: INTEGRATION

53. * A particle moves in the xy-plane so that its velocity at any time t, $0 \leq t \leq 2\pi$, is given by $\dfrac{dx}{dt} = 5\sin\frac{t}{2}$, $\dfrac{dy}{dt} = \ln 5t$. At time $t = 1$, the particle is at the point $(7,2)$. Find the y-coordinate of the position of the particle at time $t = 3$.

144

54. Let R be the region in the first and fourth quadrants bounded by the graph of $y = \ln(x^2 + 1)$ the line $y = -4x$, and the vertical line $x = 3$. Write, but do not evaluate, an expression involving one or more integrals that gives the perimeter of R.

55. The arc length for the graph of the differentiable function g between $x = 0$ and $x = 2$ is 11. Define the function k by $k(x) = 5g\left(\frac{x}{5}\right)$. Find the arc length of the graph of $y = k(x)$ from $x = 0$ to $x = 10$.

56. $\int_1^\infty \frac{x}{x^4+1} dx =$

57. * A particle moves in the xy-plane so that its velocity at any time t, $0 < t < 2\pi$, is given by $\frac{dx}{dt} = 5\sin\frac{t}{2}$, $\frac{dy}{dt} = \ln 5t$. Find the total distance traveled by the particle over the time interval $0 < t < 2\pi$.

58. Consider the polar equations $r = \sqrt{2}$ and $r = 2\cos\theta$. Let D be the region in the first quadrant bounded by the graphs of the two equations and the x-axis. Set up an expression involving one or more integrals with respect to the polar angle θ that represents the area of D.

LEVEL 4: SERIES

59. A function h has derivatives of all orders at $x = 2$. Let $P_n(x)$ denote the nth-degree Taylor polynomial for h about $x = 2$. It is known that $h(2) = -1$, $h''(2) = -\frac{1}{2}$, $h'''(2) = 3$, and $P_1(1) = -3$. Find $h'(2)$ and $P_3(x)$.

60. The Taylor series for a function h about $x = 2$ is given by $\sum_{n=1}^{\infty} \frac{(-1)^n 5^n}{\sqrt{n^3}}(x - 1)^n$ and converges to $h(x)$ for $|x - 1| < \frac{1}{5}$. Find the first four nonzero terms and the general term of the Taylor series for h', the derivative of h, about $x = 1$. Find the interval of convergence of the Taylor series for h'.

61. Write the first five nonzero terms of the Maclaurin series for $g(x) = x^2 e^{x^3} + 2x\cos x^2$. The find the value of $g^{(11)}(0)$.

62. Let $g(x) = \cos(x^3) + \sin 2x$. Write the first four nonzero terms of the Maclaurin series for $g'(x^3)$.

145

63. * Let $g(x) = \cos(x^3) + \sin 2x$. Use the first four nonzero terms of the Maclaurin series for $k(x) = \int_0^x g'(u^3)\,du$ to approximate $k(1)$.

$$h(x) = \begin{cases} \dfrac{\cos x - 1}{x} & \text{for } x \neq 0 \\ 0 & \text{for } x = 0 \end{cases}$$

64. The function h, defined above, has derivatives of all orders. Define the function k by $k(x) = 2 + \int_0^x h(u)\,du$. Write the sixth degree Taylor polynomial for k about $x = 0$, and then estimate the value of $k(1)$ to 5 decimal place accuracy.

LEVEL 5: FREE RESPONSE QUESTIONS

* 65 – 70 For $t \geq 1$, a particle is moving along a curve so that its position at time t is $(x(t), y(t))$. At time $t = 2$, the particle is at position (1,3). It is known that $\dfrac{dx}{dt} = \dfrac{\ln t}{\sqrt{t}}$ and $\dfrac{dy}{dt} = \sin^2 t$.

65. * Is the horizontal movement of the particle left or right at time $t = 2$? Justify your answer. Find the slope of the path of the particle at time $t = 2$.

66. * Find the y-coordinate of the particle's position at time $t = \dfrac{\pi}{2}$.

67. * Find the speed of the particle at time $t = \dfrac{\pi}{2}$.

68. * Find the acceleration vector of the particle at time $t = \dfrac{\pi}{2}$.

69. * Find the distance traveled by the particle from time $t = \dfrac{\pi}{2}$ to $t = 2$.

70. * Find the time t, $1 \leq t \leq 4$, when the line tangent to the path of the particle is horizontal. Is the direction of the motion of the particle to the left or right at that time. Justify your answer.

71 – 76 The polar curves r_1 and r_2 are given by $r_1(\theta) = 6$ and $r_2(\theta) = 8 - 4\cos\theta$.

71. Sketch the graphs of r_1 and r_2, and shade the region D that is inside both the graphs of r_1 and r_2.

146

72. Find the area of the region D that is inside both the graphs of r_1 and r_2.

73. For the curve r_2, find the value of $\frac{dx}{d\theta}$ at $\theta = \frac{\pi}{3}$.

74. The distance between r_1 and r_2 changes for $0 \le \theta \le 2\pi$. Find the rate at which the distance between the two curves is changing with respect to θ when $\theta = \frac{\pi}{6}$.

75. A particle moves along the curve r_2 so that $\frac{d\theta}{dt} = 5$ for all times $t \ge 0$. Find the value of $\frac{dr_2}{dt}$ at $\theta = \frac{\pi}{6}$.

76. * A particle moves along the curve r_2 so that at time t, $\theta = 2t^3$. Find the time t in the interval $0 \le t \le 1$ for which the y-coordinate of the particle's position is 3. Then find the particle's position and velocity vectors in terms of t.

77 – 80 The function h has a Taylor series about $x = 5$ that converges to $h(x)$ for all x in the interval of convergence. The nth derivative of h at $x = 5$ is given by $h^{(n)}(5) = \frac{(-1)^n 2^n (n+1)!}{n 3^n}$ for $n \ge 1$, and $h(5) = 1$.

77. Write the first four terms and the general term of the Taylor series for h about $x = 5$.

78. Find the radius of convergence for the Taylor series for h about $x = 5$. Justify your answer.

79. Find the interval of convergence for the Taylor series for h about $x = 5$. Justify your answer.

80. Let H be a function satisfying $H(5) = -6$ and $H'(x) = h(x)$ for all x. Write the first four terms and the general term of the Taylor series for H about $x = 5$. Does this Taylor series converge at $x = 3$?

147

SUPPLEMENTAL BC PROBLEMS
ANSWERS

LEVEL 1: DIFFERENTIATION

1. $\frac{1}{3}\left(\frac{\sqrt{x}}{2(x+1)} + \arctan\sqrt{x}\right)$
2. $\frac{3\sqrt{2}}{8}$
3. $\frac{3t\sqrt{1-t^4}}{2}$
4. $\langle 2, -4 \rangle$

LEVEL 1: INTEGRATION

5. -2
6. 2.097 or 2.098
7. $\frac{\pi^2}{8}$
8. $1 + \ln\sqrt{\frac{3}{2}}$
9. .185
10. 14

LEVEL 1: SERIES

11. $\frac{5}{3}$
12. C
13. C
14. A
15. E
16. $-\frac{1}{3} \leq x \leq \frac{1}{3}$

LEVEL 2: DIFFERENTIATION

17. $y - 1 = -2e(x - e)$ or $y = -2ex + 2e^2 + 1$
18. $y = e$
19. 7.389
20. A

LEVEL 2: INTEGRATION

21. $2\sqrt{3}$
22. $\ln(\sqrt{2} + 1)$
23. $(x^2 - 2x + 2)e^x + C$
24. π
25. $(-2, 0)$
26. 10π

LEVEL 2: SERIES

27. E
28. 3
29. E
30. [3,7)
31. $\ln 3 - x - \dfrac{x^2}{2} - \dfrac{x^3}{3}$
32. D

LEVEL 3: DIFFERENTIATION

33. A
34. $\dfrac{35}{3}$, 11.666, or 11.667
35. D
36. 6.574 or 6.575

LEVEL 3: INTEGRATION

37. D
38. A
39. B
40. 5
41. $8 + \pi + 3\sqrt{3}$
42. $\frac{2}{13}e^{2x}\sin 3x - \frac{3}{13}e^{2x}\cos 3x + C$

LEVEL 3: SERIES

43. $\frac{1}{60}$
44. D
45. $1 - \frac{5^2}{2!} + \frac{5^4}{4!} - \frac{5^6}{6!}$
46. .2955
47. $R = \frac{1}{4}, I = [\frac{11}{4}, \frac{13}{4}]$
48. $h(x) = -\frac{x}{2!} + \frac{x^3}{4!} - \frac{x^5}{6!} + \frac{x^7}{8!} - \frac{x^9}{10!} + \cdots + \frac{(-1)^n x^{2n-1}}{(2n)!} + \cdots$

From the Maclaurin series for h we have $h'(0) = -\frac{1}{2!} = -\frac{1}{2}$. So $x = 0$ is *not* a critical number for h, and therefore h *does not* have a relative extremum at $x = 0$.

LEVEL 4: DIFFERENTIATION

49. $\frac{dy}{dt} \approx -421.910$. The y-coordinate of the particle is decreasing at a rate of 421.91.
50. .320
51. $\langle -\frac{5}{4}, -\frac{1}{\pi^2} \rangle$
52. For $a < \theta < b$, the length of the radius r is increasing. Therefore the curve gets farther from the origin as the angle θ increases from a to b.

LEVEL 4: INTEGRATION

53. 6.514 or 6.515

54. $3\sqrt{17} + 12 + \ln 10 + \int_0^3 \sqrt{1 + \frac{4x^2}{(x^2+1)^2}}\, dx$

55. 55

56. $\frac{\pi}{8}$

57. 26.348

58. Area $= \frac{1}{2}\int_0^{\frac{\pi}{4}}\left(\sqrt{2}\right)^2 d\theta + \frac{1}{2}\int_{\frac{\pi}{4}}^{\frac{\pi}{2}}(2\cos\theta)^2\, d\theta$

LEVEL 4: SERIES

59. $h'(2) = 2$

$\qquad P_3(x) = -1 + 2(x-2) - \frac{1}{4}(x-2)^2 + \frac{1}{2}(x-2)^3$

60. The first four terms of the Taylor series for h' are

$\qquad -5 + \frac{25}{\sqrt{2}}(x-1) - \frac{125}{\sqrt{3}}(x-1)^2 + \frac{625}{2}(x-1)^3$

The general term of the Taylor series for h' is

$\frac{(-1)^n 5^n}{\sqrt{n}}(x-1)^{n-1}$ for $n \geq 1$

$I = \left(\frac{4}{5}, \frac{6}{5}\right]$

61. $g(x) \approx 2x + x^2 + \frac{x^8}{2} + \frac{x^9}{12} + \frac{x^{11}}{6}$, $g^{(11)}(0) = 6{,}652{,}800$

62. $2 - 4x^6 + \frac{4}{3}x^{12} - 3x^{15}$

63. $\frac{5869}{4368}$ or 1.343 or 1.344

64. $P_6(x) = 2 - \frac{x^2}{2\cdot 2!} + \frac{x^4}{4\cdot 4!} - \frac{x^6}{6\cdot 6!}$, $k(1) \approx 1.76019$

LEVEL 5: FREE RESPONSE QUESTIONS

65. $\frac{dx}{dt}\Big|_{t=2} = \frac{\ln 2}{\sqrt{2}} > 0$. So the particle is moving right at time

$\qquad t = 2$.

$\qquad$ slope $= 1.686$ or 1.687

66. 2.596

151

67. 1.062 or 1.063

68. ⟨.393,0⟩

69. .444 or .445

70. $t = \pi$

Since $x'(\pi) = \dfrac{\ln \pi}{\sqrt{\pi}} > 0$, the particle is moving to the right at time $t = \pi$

71.

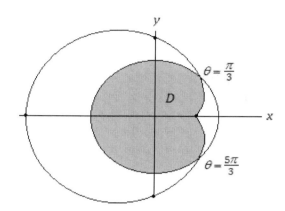

72. Area $= 24\pi + \int_0^{\frac{\pi}{3}}(8 - 4\cos\theta)^2 \, d\theta = 48\pi - 30\sqrt{3}$

73. $-2\sqrt{3}$

74. 2

75. 10

76. $y(t) = 3$ when $t = .693$

Position vector $= \langle x(t), y(t) \rangle =$
$\langle (8 - 4\cos(2t^3))\cos(2t^3), (8 - 4\cos(2t^3))\sin(2t^3) \rangle$

Velocity vector $= \langle x'(t), y'(t) \rangle =$
$\langle 48t^2 \sin(2t^3)(\cos(2t^3) - 1), 24t^2(2\cos(2t^3) - \cos(4t^3)) \rangle$

77. $h(x) = 1 - \dfrac{4}{3}(x - 5) + \dfrac{2}{3}(x - 5)^2 - \dfrac{32}{81}(x - 5)^3 + \cdots +$
$\dfrac{(-1)^n(n+1)2^n}{n3^n}(x - 5)^n + \cdots$

78. $\lim_{n \to \infty}\left| \dfrac{\frac{(n+2)2^{n+1}}{(n+1)3^{n+1}}(x-5)^{n+1}}{\frac{(n+1)2^n}{n3^n}(x-5)^n} \right| = \dfrac{2}{3}|x - 5|$ which is less than 1 when
$|x - 5| < \dfrac{3}{2}$. So $R = \dfrac{3}{2}$.

79. $|x - 5| < \frac{3}{2}$ is equivalent to $\frac{7}{2} < x < \frac{13}{2}$.

When $x = \frac{7}{2}$, the series is $\sum_{n=0}^{\infty} \frac{n+1}{n}$ which diverges by the divergence test.

When $x = \frac{13}{2}$, the series is $\sum_{n=0}^{\infty} (-1)^n \frac{n+1}{n}$ which also diverges by the divergence test.

So $I = (\frac{7}{2}, \frac{13}{2})$.

80. $H(x) = -6 + (x - 5) - \frac{2}{3}(x - 5)^2 + \frac{2}{9}(x - 5)^3$

$+ \cdots + \frac{(-1)^{n-1} 2^{n-1}}{(n-1)3^{n-1}}(x - 5)^n + \cdots$

This Taylor series does not converge at $x = 3$.

ACTIONS TO COMPLETE AFTER YOU HAVE READ THIS BOOK

1. Continue to practice AP Calculus problems for 20 to 30 minutes each day

Keep practicing problems of the appropriate levels until two days before the exam.

2. Use my Forum page for additional help

If you feel you need extra help that you cannot get from this book, please feel free to post your questions in the AP Calculus section of my forum at

www.satprepget800.com/forum

3. Review this book

If this book helped you, please post your positive feedback on the site you purchased it from; e.g. Amazon, Barnes and Noble, etc.

4. Sign up for free updates

If you have not done so yet, visit the following webpage and enter your email address to receive updates and supplementary materials for free including detailed solutions to all the AP Calculus AB problems in this book.

www.thesatmathprep.com/320APCalSup.html

About the Author

Steve Warner, a New York native, earned his Ph.D. at Rutgers University in Pure Mathematics in May, 2001. While a graduate student, Dr. Warner won the TA Teaching Excellence Award.

After Rutgers, Dr. Warner joined the Penn State Mathematics Department as an Assistant Professor. In September, 2002, Dr. Warner returned to New York to accept an Assistant Professor position at Hofstra University. By September 2007, Dr. Warner had received tenure and was promoted to Associate Professor. He has taught undergraduate and graduate courses in Precalculus, Calculus, Linear Algebra, Differential Equations, Mathematical Logic, Set Theory and Abstract Algebra.

Over that time, Dr. Warner participated in a five year NSF grant, "The MSTP Project," to study and improve mathematics and science curriculum in poorly performing junior high schools. He also published several articles in scholarly journals, specifically on Mathematical Logic.

Dr. Warner has over 15 years of experience in general math tutoring and over 10 years of experience in AP Calculus tutoring. He has tutored students both individually and in group settings.

In February, 2010 Dr. Warner released his first SAT prep book "The 32 Most Effective SAT Math Strategies." The second edition of this book was released in January, 2011. In February, 2012 Dr. Warner released his second SAT prep book "320 SAT Math Problems arranged by Topic and Difficulty Level." Between September 2012 and January 2013 Dr. Warner released his three book series "28 SAT Math Lessons to Improve Your Score in One Month." In June, 2013 Dr. Warner released the "SAT Prep Official Study Guide Math Companion." In November, 2013 Dr. Warner released the "ACT Prep Red Book – 320 Math Problems With Solutions." Between May 2014 and July 2014 Dr. Warner released "320 SAT Math Subject Test Problems arranged by Topic and Difficulty Level." for the Level 1 and Level 2 tests. In November, 2014 Dr. Warner released "320 AP Calculus AB Problems arranged by Topic and Difficulty Level."

BOOKS BY DR. STEVE WARNER

 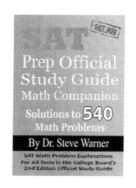 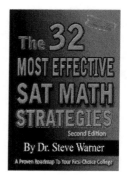

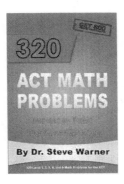

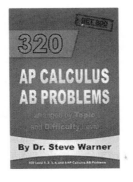

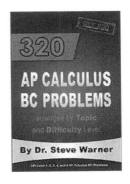

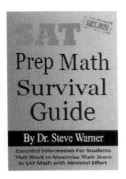

Made in the USA
San Bernardino, CA
16 October 2017